CREATIVE USES · FOR RECYCLABLES ·

175 Easy-to-Do
HALLOWEEN
CRAFTS

Edited by Sharon Dunn Umnik

BOYDS MILLS PRESS

Inside this book...
you'll find a fabulous assortment of crafts made from recyclable items and inexpensive things found in or around your house. Have pencils, crayons, scissors, tape, paintbrushes, and other supplies for craft making close by.

When you're trick-or-treating, practice Halloween safety: Always trick-or-treat with an adult or a group of friends. As you go to friends' homes, take off your mask, or slide it to the top of your head so you can see clearly.– *the Editor*

Copyright © 1995 by Boyds Mills Press
All rights reserved

Published by Bell Books
Boyds Mills Press, Inc.
A Highlights Company
815 Church Street
Honesdale, Pennsylvania 18431
Printed in the United States of America

Publisher Cataloging-in-Publication Data
175 easy-to-do Halloween crafts : creative uses for recyclables /
edited by Sharon Dunn Umnik.—1st ed.
[64]p. : col. ill. ; cm.
Summary : Includes step-by-step directions to make
Halloween masks, decorations, cards, and more. Also includes
instructions for decorating pumpkins.
ISBN 1-56397-372-3
1. Handicraft—Juvenile literature. 2. Halloween decorations—
Juvenile literature. 3. Recycling (Waste)—Juvenile literature.
[1. Handicraft. 2. Halloween. 3. Recycling (Waste).]
I. Umnik, Sharon Dunn. II. Title.
745.5—dc20   1995   CIP
Library of Congress Catalog Card Number 94-79157

First edition, 1995
Book designed by Charlie Cary
The text of this book is set in 11-point New Century Schoolbook.

10 9 8 7 6

Craft Contributors: Caroline Arnold, Barbara Baker, Katherine Corliss Bartow, B. J. Benish, Bea Blasing, Linda Bloomgren, Doris D. Breiholz, Mindy Cherez, Kathleen Conrad, Liby Croce, Sandra E. Csippan, Patti DeLotell, Ruth Dougherty, Paige Matthews Eckard, Kathy Everett, Deanna Fendler, Tanya Turner Fry, Julie Fultz, Roberta Glatz, Alice Gilbreath, Connie Giunta, Mavis Grant, Evelyn Green, Janet Grottodden, Jean Hale, Edna Harrington, Barbara Albers Hill, Velma Flower Holt, Loretta Holz, Carmen Horn, Tama Kain, Shirley Kallus, Garnett C. Kooker, Sylvia Kreng, Virginia L. Kroll, Ella L. Langenberg, Lee Lindeman, Jean Lyon, Agnes Maddy, Jo Ann Markway, Betty Merritt, Evelyn Minshull, June Rose Mobly, Mary Lou Murphy, James W. Perrin Jr., Deanna Peters, Jean Reynolds, Terry A. Ricioli, Jean F. Roath, Kathy Ross, Vivian Smallowitz, Andrew J. Smith, Beth Tobler, Sharon Dunn Umnik, Bernice Walz, Bonnie Wedge, Margaret Joque Williams, Agnes Choate Wonson, Jinx Woolson.

Balloon Goblins

These Halloween decorations may be used either as large party favors set on top of a paper cup or as party decorations. They can be hung from the ceiling or doorway. (Remember that balloons are fragile. Even with care one may pop as you work on it and give you a Halloween scare! Be sure to clean up any broken pieces of balloon and throw them away immediately.)

PUMPKIN

(balloon, poster board, construction paper)

1. Cut a base for the pumpkin from a piece of poster board.

2. Blow up a balloon and knot the end. Roll a piece of tape, secure it to the balloon, and attach the balloon to the base.

3. Cut features from black construction paper, and tape in place with small strips of rolled transparent tape. Cut a stem from green construction paper, and tape to the top of the balloon.

CAT

(balloon, plastic-foam cup, construction paper, permanent marker)

1. Blow up a balloon and knot the end.

2. Attach a piece of tape to the inside of a plastic-foam cup, leaving half of it bent like a tab over the opening of the cup. Do the same on the opposite edge of the cup.

3. Place the balloon with the knotted end inside the cup. The tabs of tape should hold it in place. Tape the cup to the work surface to hold the balloon upright.

4. Cut ears, eyes, nose, mouth, and bow tie from construction paper, and attach with pieces of rolled transparent tape. Add whiskers and eyelashes with a permanent marker.

OWL

(balloon, construction paper, permanent marker, string)

1. Blow up a balloon and knot the end.

2. Cut a large V shape from black construction paper. Cut eyes from pieces of black and white paper and the beak from orange paper. Attach to the balloon with pieces of rolled transparent tape.

3. Draw feathers on the balloon with a permanent marker.

4. Tie a string around the knotted end of the balloon, and hang the owl where it can swing in the breeze.

Real Pumpkin Heads

These pumpkins are fun because they are created with many different materials. Use plastic rings cut from food containers to make necks for some of the pumpkins.

SWEET SUE
(pumpkin, two copper scouring pads, toothpick halves, felt, pompons, lace)

1. For the hair, stretch two copper scouring pads over the top of a pumpkin. Hold in place with toothpick halves.

2. Cut eyes, a nose, a mouth, cheeks, and ears from felt. Roll pieces of tape and attach to the back of the features. Press the features in place. Glue a pompon on each ear lobe for an earring.

3. Add a felt-and-lace bow to the hair. Hold in place with a toothpick half. Wrap a strip of lace around the neck.

PAINTED PAT
(pumpkin, poster paint)

1. On a piece of paper, sketch a face for your pumpkin. Then lightly draw it on the pumpkin itself.

2. Paint the features with poster paint and let dry. You may want to go over the features a second time.

3. Display the pumpkin inside a window where it is dry.

VEGGIE VERN
(pumpkin, table knife, two apples, cucumber, toothpick halves, marshmallows, paper, celery)

1. Have an adult help you when using a knife. Cut two apples and a cucumber in half. On the pumpkin surface, trace around one top-half section of the apple for the mouth, two bottom-half sections of the apples for the cheeks, and one half of the cucumber for the nose. Cut around the tracings with a table knife, cutting through the pumpkin wall, and push the apple halves and cucumber inside the pumpkin.

2. Insert two whole toothpicks where the eyes should be, and place a marshmallow on each one. Add a pupil to each eye made from paper. For the eyebrows, cut small sections from the leftover cucumber and attach them with toothpick halves.

3. Cut the leafy sections from a bunch of celery. Attach them with toothpick halves to the top of the pumpkin to make hair.

WENDY WITCH
(pumpkin, construction paper, fabric)

1. On construction paper, draw a large circle with a smaller one inside to make the hat brim. Cut out the small circle, cutting tabs along the inside edge of the doughnut shape. To make the hat top, draw a circle on another piece of paper. Cut off about half of the circle and save for features. Roll the other section into a cone shape, fitting it over the tabs of the brim and taping in place.

2. Cut strips of paper and tape inside the hat for hair. Place the hat on top of the pumpkin. Cut out facial features, and attach with rolled pieces of tape.

3. Add a piece of fabric around the witch's neck.

TOPPER DAN
(pumpkin, cotton balls, plastic lids and tops, teaspoon, paper, poster board, chenille sticks, fabric)

1. For hair, brush glue around the top of the pumpkin and press cotton balls into it.

2. On the pumpkin surface, trace around two plastic lids for eyes, a plastic top for the nose, and a plastic lid for the mouth with a pencil. Using a teaspoon, dig out shallow holes within the traced circles. Twist the lids or tops into the holes.

3. Cut out pupils from paper, and glue them on the eyes. Cut out a mustache shape from a piece of poster board, and cover it with cotton. Trim around the edges with scissors if needed. Glue the mustache between the nose and mouth.

4. Twist two chenille sticks together to make eyeglasses, and place the earpieces snugly in the hair. Cut two ears from large plastic lids. Have an adult help you cut a slot on each side of the head, and insert the ears. Use a strip of fabric for a bow tie.

CARVED CAROLINE
(pumpkin, table knife, spoons)

1. With the help of an adult, use a table knife to cut around the stem of the pumpkin and remove the top. With a large spoon, scoop out the seeds and inner membranes of the pumpkin. (Save the seeds and roast them later.)

2. On a piece of paper, sketch a face for your pumpkin. Then lightly draw it on the pumpkin itself.

3. With an adult's help cut out entire sections of the pumpkin. Or cut just below the skin surface and scoop out with a small spoon.

4. Place a small light in the center of the pumpkin to make it shine at night.

PUMPKIN CHAIN
(construction paper, permanent marker, ribbon)

1. Stack four or more pieces of orange paper. (The more pieces of paper, the more pumpkin shapes, and the longer the chain.) Place a pumpkin shape on top of the stack, and cut around it.

2. Using a permanent black marker, draw only eyes and mouths on the pumpkins. Leave room in the middle, where the nose will be, to cut two vertical slits in each pumpkin.

3. Make a pumpkin chain by weaving a long piece of ribbon through the slits in each pumpkin.

SPOOKY MOON MOBILE
(heavy cardboard plates, poster paint, facial tissue, string, construction paper)

1. Cut two crescent moon shapes from heavy cardboard plates. Paint them yellow inside and out and let dry.

2. Place the moon shapes together, with the plate bottoms toward the outside, and staple them along the curved edges.

3. To make a ghost, tightly crumple a white tissue into a ball. Place it in the middle of a second tissue, and pull the tissue smoothly around the ball. Tie it at the neck with string. Glue on paper eyes.

4. Make pumpkins the same way as the ghost, but cut off the tissue to make a stem. Paint the pumpkins orange and the stems green. Add a paper face.

5. Cut bats from paper. Punch two holes in the centers, and tie a long string through them.

6. Punch holes along the inner curve of the moon. Tie the strings from the ghosts, pumpkins, and bats to the holes. Punch another hole in the top of the moon and attach a string for a hanger.

CAT HAND PUPPET
(sock, thread, felt)

1. Gather material on each side of the toe portion of a sock for the ears. Tie the ears with thread.

2. Cut out eyes and whiskers from felt, and glue them in place on the foot of the sock.

3. Place your hand inside the sock to make your cat perform.

GHOST PIN
(white felt, permanent marker, safety pin)

1. Cut two matching ghost shapes from white felt. Glue them together and let them dry.

2. With a permanent marker, draw on the ghost's face and outline the body.

3. Glue a safety pin to the back of the ghost. Then glue a small strip of felt across the opened pin and let it dry.

HALLOWEEN TABLE DECORATION
(cereal box, two toothpaste boxes, construction paper, yarn)

1. Cover a cereal box and two toothpaste boxes with construction paper.

2. Cut off two corners of each toothpaste box at an angle, and glue the boxes to the bottom of the cereal box for feet.

3. Cut features from paper, and glue on yarn for hair.

PAPER-PLATE SPIDER
(black paper, two small paper plates, poster paint, string)

1. Cut eight long strips of black paper for the spider's legs and a circle for the spider's head.

2. Glue the two small paper plates together, plate bottoms facing out, with the legs and head placed between the edges.

3. Paint the body black. Glue a long piece of string to the middle of the back so the spider can dangle from the ceiling of your room.

CORNCOB WITCH

(corncob with husk, paint, dried beans, paper, lightweight cardboard)

1. Remove the kernels from a dried corncob and trim the ends. Paint the body black except for the head. Glue on dried beans for eyes, a nose, and a mouth. Trim the cornhusks for the hair.

2. To make the hat, cut two circles from black paper. Cut the center out of one circle. Cut a slit to the center of the other circle and roll it into the shape of a cone. Glue the cone shape onto the flat circle, covering the hole. Glue the hat to the cornhusk hair.

3. Attach a cardboard base of black feet so that the witch can stand.

YARN JACK-O'-LANTERN

(plastic food container, glue, water, balloon, orange yarn)

1. In a plastic food container, make a mixture of equal amounts of white glue and water.

2. Blow up a balloon and knot the end. Tie a piece of string around the knot.

3. Dip orange yarn into the glue-and-water mixture. Wrap the yarn around the balloon. Hang the balloon until the yarn has dried.

4. Pop the balloon and carefully pull it through the strands of yarn. Cut and glue paper features to the yarn pumpkin.

HAUNTED-HOUSE CARD

(construction paper)

1. Fold a piece of construction paper in half. Draw a house with windows and doors on the front of the card. Cut around three sides of each window and the door so they will open and close.

2. Open the card and glue a piece of white paper inside, then glue the card shut.

3. Open all the windows and the door and write messages behind them or draw scary pictures. Close them up and send your card to a friend.

HALLOWEEN HANG-UP
(round cardboard container, poster paint, construction paper, yarn)

1. Cut off the bottom of a round cardboard container. Trim the container to form a cat shape, as shown. Cover it with poster paint and let dry.

2. Cut features from construction paper and glue in place.

3. Punch a hole on opposite sides of the cat shape, and tie a piece of yarn for a hanger.

GOBLIN POP-UP
(poster board, yarn, tongue depressor, plastic-foam cup, paper)

1. Cut a goblin head from poster board. Add yarn hair and other features from paper. Glue the head to one end of a tongue depressor.

2. Push the other end of the tongue depressor through the bottom of a plastic-foam cup so the goblin is hiding inside the cup. Add paper decorations to the outside of the cup.

3. Hold the stick with one hand and the cup with the other. Make the goblin pop in and out of the cup.

BAT HAT
(two 9-inch paper plates, small brown paper bag, scrap newspaper, black paper, yarn)

1. Cut the center out of one paper plate without cutting through the rim. Cut another paper plate from the edge to the center.

2. Pull the cut edges together to form a cone shape and tape. Glue the cone to the rim. Poke a hole on each side and add yarn for ties.

3. Stuff a small paper bag with scrap newspaper. Fold down and staple the top of the bag. Cut a round hole in the bottom of the bag. Add glue to the rest of the bag bottom, and press the bag onto the cone so the point of the cone is in the hole.

4. Cut wings, feet, eyes, and a mouth from black paper and glue in place.

FABRIC PUMPKIN CENTERPIECE
(fabric, pizza pan, needle and thread)

1. Place a pizza pan on a piece of orange fabric. Trace around it with a pencil and cut out the circle.

2. Sew around the edge of the circle using long stitches. When you get all the way around, pull the thread ends to gather the fabric, leaving a small hole in the center.

3. Stuff old fabric scraps into the hole, forming the pumpkin shape. Roll green fabric into a stem and push it into the hole.

4. Pull the thread very tightly and secure with a few stitches. Glue on pieces of fabric to make a face.

SCARY SKELETON
(chenille sticks, paper, thread)

1. Bend a long chenille stick in half. Below the bend, twist a second chenille stick around for the arms.

2. Just below the arms, wrap a third chenille stick around the first for the body, leaving two lengths for the legs.

3. Cut out a paper head and glue it to the body. Bend back the ends of the arms and legs to make the hands and feet.

4. Add a thread loop to the head, and jiggle it to make the skeleton dance.

TREAT BOX
(milk carton, construction paper, yarn)

1. Cut the top from a milk carton, leaving an open box. Cover the sides with glue and construction paper.

2. Decorate the box with cutouts from construction paper and yarn to make funny and scary faces.

3. Punch a hole on opposite sides at the top of the box. To make a handle, thread two pieces of yarn through the holes and knot the ends.

BREAD-DOUGH WITCH NECKLACE
(slices of bread, table knife, bowl, tablespoon, white glue, mixing spoon, waxed paper, paper, poster paint, toothpick, yarn)

1. Remove the crusts from a couple of slices of bread. Tear the bread into small pieces and put them in a bowl, add a tablespoon of white glue, and mix together with a spoon. Work the dough into a ball with your hands until it is smooth and elastic.

2. Press the dough out on waxed paper. Draw and cut out a witch paper pattern. Place the pattern on the dough and cut around the witch with a table knife. Make a hole with a toothpick and let the witch dry.

3. Paint details on the witch. When dry, thread a piece of yarn through the hole for a necklace.

MILK CARTON CAT
(one-pint milk carton, poster paint, cardboard)

1. Use a one-pint milk carton for the cat, with the opened peaks forming the ears. Draw the eyes and mouth on the side of the carton and cut them out. Paint the carton and let dry. (Add a little dishwashing detergent to the paint to help make it stick to the carton, if needed.)

2. Cut a slit in the bottom of the carton below the cat's face. Cut a strip of cardboard as wide as the carton and as long as needed to reach the carton top. Place the strip in the slit and trace the eyes and mouth on it.

3. Paint the eyes on the cardboard strip. Draw a long tongue on another piece of cardboard that will fit inside the cat's mouth. Cut it out and paint it. Glue one end of the tongue to the strip of cardboard so the other end of the tongue can slide in and out of the mouth.

4. Hold the carton with one hand and the cardboard strip with the other. Make the cat's tongue and eyes move up and down.

HOOTY OWL
(paper plate, markers, construction paper)

1. Cut along the inside of the fluted edge, except for two inches on the top and bottom, as shown.

2. Fold the two cut edges inward so that they overlap, and glue them down.

3. Color the owl with markers. Cut eyes, ears, feet, and a beak from construction paper and glue them in place.

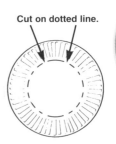

Cut on dotted line.

CAT PICTURE
(construction paper)

1. Cut construction paper into long, thin strips. Tape the strips to make a large circle for the cat's body and a smaller one for its head. Make a pumpkin the same way.

2. Add a tail, ears, and eyes to the cat.

3. Glue the circles to a spooky-looking background.

EGG-CARTON BAT BRANCH
(plastic-foam egg carton, construction paper, thread, tree branch, yarn)

1. For each bat, cut two cups from a plastic-foam egg carton. Make wings from black paper and glue them between the cups.

2. Cut pointed ears from paper and glue in place. Add paper-punch dot eyes and a mouth cut from paper.

3. Glue a thread to each bat and tie each one to a fallen tree branch. Tie pieces of yarn to the branch to hang it as a mobile.

SCRAP-HAPPY WITCH
(cardboard, fabric, yarn, felt, buttons, construction paper)

1. Draw and cut out a witch from a piece of cardboard. Glue on fabric for the face and trim around the edges. To make hair, glue loops of yarn around the witch's face.

2. Draw and cut out a hat from a piece of felt. Glue it on top of the hair. Glue on two button eyes and other facial features from fabric.

3. Decorate the hat with felt cutouts. Add a felt collar under the witch's chin. Glue a loop of yarn to the back of the witch for a hanger.

PUMPKIN NAPKIN HOLDER
(bathroom tissue tube, poster paint, permanent marker)

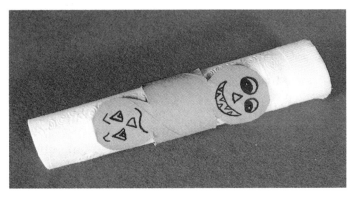

1. Measure about 1 1/2 inches in from each end of a bathroom tissue tube, and draw a pencil line around the tube.

2. At one end, draw a pumpkin from the edge of the tube to the pencil line. Draw another pumpkin at the opposite end. Then draw two more identical pumpkins on the other side of the tube.

3. Carefully cut around the pumpkin shapes and the pencil line with scissors.

4. Paint the tube and let dry. Draw features on the pumpkins, and place a rolled napkin through the middle of the tube.

• •

HALLOWEEN BERRY BASKET
(plastic berry basket, ribbon, poster board)

1. Start at a corner and weave lengths of ribbon in and out through the sections of a plastic berry basket. Tie each ribbon into a bow at the end.

2. From a piece of poster board, cut out the head of a cat with a long neck. Decorate it with other pieces of poster board and markers.

3. Cut small slits in the neck section and weave them into the berry basket sections at the corner above the bows. Fill the basket with treats.

• •

BAG OWL
(small brown paper bag, old newspaper, construction paper, self-adhesive reinforcement rings)

1. Loosely stuff a small brown paper bag half full of old crumpled newspaper.

2. Bring the top of the bag together, fold the two outside edges in toward the center, and glue to form a point.

3. Fold the point down over the other half of the bag and glue in place.

4. From construction paper, make a paper beak and glue to the point. Make feet and glue to the bottom of the bag. Add two self-adhesive reinforcement rings for eyes.

SPOOKY SEE-THROUGH
(glue, food coloring, plastic food wrap, construction paper)

1. Mix a few drops of food coloring into white glue to make paint. Paint a picture on a piece of plastic food wrap. While it is still wet, cover your painting with another sheet of plastic food wrap. Press the plastic together.

2. Cut strips of construction paper, and glue them around the edges for a frame.

3. Add a loop of yarn to the back for a hanger. Hang the picture in a window where the light will filter through it.

OWL CANDY BOX
(construction paper, self-adhesive reinforcement rings, cardboard egg carton)

1. Draw the owl pattern, as shown, on a square piece of construction paper.

2. Cut out the owl pattern and fold along the dotted lines, as shown in the pattern. Tape the sides together to form a box.

3. Add reinforcement rings for eyes. Glue on paper pupils and paper beaks. Fill with treats.

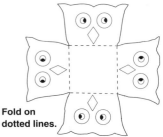

Fold on dotted lines.

EGG-CARTON PUMPKINS
(cardboard egg carton, poster paint, construction paper)

1. Cut six cups from a cardboard egg carton. Glue them together in pairs to make three pumpkins. Paint them orange.

2. Cut a section of three peaks from the egg carton for the base. Trim two peaks for different heights. Paint the base black.

3. Glue the pumpkins to the base. Attach cut-paper features to the pumpkins.

JACK-O'-LANTERN FAVOR
(plastic margarine tub, construction paper, chenille stick)

1. Wash and dry a plastic margarine tub and lid.

2. Cut out a paper circle to fit the top of the lid. Cut out eyes, a nose, and a mouth from the paper circle, and glue it to the lid. Color the pupils in the eyes and add a stem from paper.

3. Punch two holes, about 1/4 inch apart, near the top rim of the tub; then punch a second pair of holes 2 inches away from the first set.

4. Push each end of a chenille stick through the pairs of holes and twist together, making a handle.

BOTTLE WITCH
(1-liter plastic beverage bottle, 2 1/2-inch plastic-foam ball, poster board, lightweight cotton cloth, ribbon, sequins, black paper, self-adhesive stars)

1. Remove the top of a 1-liter plastic beverage bottle, and spread glue around the inside and outside of the spout. Twist and press a 2 1/2-inch plastic-foam ball into the spout for the head.

2. Draw and cut shoes from a piece of poster board, and glue them to the bottom of the bottle.

3. Cut a 24-inch round piece of lightweight cotton cloth. Cut a slit to the middle. Spread glue around the neck of the bottle and wrap the cloth around it, adding more glue if needed. Tie a piece of ribbon around the neck.

4. To make hair, cut and glue strips of cloth to the ball. For the face, cut features from cloth and glue in place. Add sequins for eyes.

5. To make the hat, cut two circles from black paper. Cut the center out of one circle. Cut a slit to the center of the other circle, and roll it into the shape of a cone. Glue the cone shape onto the flat circle, covering the hole. Then glue the hat to the head.

6. Add self-adhesive stars to the hat and cloth.

MOUSE HAT
(construction paper, chenille stick)

1. Cut out a 9-inch square of construction paper for the hat. Fold it into a triangle.

2. To make the band, cut a strip of paper 11 1/2 inches long and 1 1/2 inches wide. Staple the band to each of the corners opposite the fold.

3. Glue on features made from circles of cut paper. For the tail, staple a curled chenille stick to the top corner.

Hand Masks

*Here are simple hand masks to create and carry with you
while trick-or-treating.*

PIGGY
(heavy cardboard, thread spool, wooden tongue depressor, poster paint)

1. Draw and cut out two 9-inch circles, one from heavy cardboard and one from pink construction paper. Cut two ears from pink paper, and glue them to the cardboard circle. Glue the pink circle to the front of the cardboard circle.

2. Draw two circles for the pig's eyes, and cut them out. Glue on a thread spool for the snout. Use a marker to draw on a mouth and add other details.

3. Paint a wooden tongue depressor and let it dry. Glue the tongue depressor to one side of the pig's head to use as a holder.

CAT
(platter, poster board, paper, paint stir-stick)

1. Cut out a platter shape from a piece of black poster board. Cut a slit to the center, as shown. Pull one edge of the slit over the top of the other to raise the center slightly. Glue to hold it in place.

2. To make the eyes, cut shapes from paper. Glue one on top of the other, and then glue in place on the mask. Cut holes in the center of each paper eye. Add ears, whiskers, and a mouth made from paper. Add a paper bow tie.

3. Glue a paint stir-stick to the inside of the mask for a handle.

Cut

TROPICAL BIRD
(corrugated cardboard, tempera paint, paper, two tongue depressors, yarn)

1. Ask an adult to help you cut out the mask shape and holes for eyes, as shown in the diagram, from corrugated cardboard. Paint one side of the mask, making a beak with a different color.

2. Cut feather-shaped pieces of paper, and glue them around the mask. Roll strips of paper, and glue them around the eyes.

3. Glue two tongue depressors together, overlapping two ends, and let dry. Glue one end to the back of the mask for a handle. Criss-cross yarn from one end of the handle to the other and glue in place, leaving the ends hanging down.

PANDA
(heavy paper plate, construction paper, lightweight cardboard, poster paint, paper towel tube)

1. Draw a panda face on the bottom of a heavy white paper plate. Cut out holes for eyes and a small mouth. Glue a red tongue cut from construction paper near the mouth.

2. Cut ears from lightweight cardboard and paint them black. Staple them to the plate with the smooth section of the staple inside.

3. Cover a paper towel tube with black construction paper and fasten with tape. Staple the tube to one side of the panda face for a handle.

CATERPILLAR
(heavy paper plates, poster paint, poster board, yarn)

1. Paint the bottoms of heavy paper plates with poster paint and let dry.

2. Make a face on one plate with pieces of poster board and glue. Cut out holes for the eyes, draw eyelashes, and staple on antennae.

3. Cut legs from poster board and staple them opposite each other on the plates. Add dots cut from poster board.

4. To connect the body, punch two holes, about 1 inch apart, at the edge of the plate where the neck would be. Punch two holes in another plate so the holes will line up. Place the holes over each other and tie with a piece of yarn. Do the same with the rest of the plates.

5. Cut a 1 1/2-inch section from the center of a plate. Cut in half, overlap, and staple together. Attach the handle over the neck area on the underside.

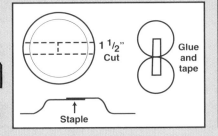

1 1/2"
Cut

Glue and tape

Staple

ELEPHANT
(four rectangular facial tissue boxes, masking tape, plastic gloves, white and black shoe polish, cloth, paper, paint stir-stick)

1. Measure 1 inch up from the bottom of three rectangular facial tissue boxes and draw a line. Cut on the line. Discard the tops.

2. Glue two boxes at right angles to one box to form the head. Cut and glue a trunk from the remaining box in place.

3. Cut the side boxes in the shape of ears. Cover the head and the ears with pieces of torn masking tape.

4. Cover your work space and wear plastic gloves. Mix black and white shoe polish together to make a gray color. Wipe the polish on the tape with a cloth.

5. Glue on large paper eyes. Cut out eyeholes. Glue on a paint stir-stick.

ROCKY PUMPKIN
(rock, yarn, felt)

1. Find the best sitting position for the rock you have chosen.

2. Starting at the bottom, squeeze glue on the rock and wrap yarn around it. Add more glue and yarn until the entire rock is covered. Let dry.

3. Cut the eyes, nose, and mouth from felt and glue them to the rock to make the jack-o'-lantern's face. Add a stem to the top.

HALLOWEEN STICK PUPPET
(construction paper, wooden tongue depressor)

1. To make the body of the witch, cut pieces of construction paper, and glue them to a wooden tongue depressor. Add hands, feet, hair, and facial features cut from paper.

2. Hold the tongue depressor in your hand and soar your witch through the air.

PLASTIC-FOAM NECKLACE
(plastic-foam tray, permanent marker,
self-adhesive reinforcement rings, yarn)

1. Draw and cut out ghosts from a white plastic-foam tray. Add facial features with a marker.

2. Place a self-adhesive reinforcement ring at the top, on the front and back of each ghost, so the holes are lined up.

3. Thread a long piece of yarn through each hole and tie a knot. Do this for each ghost.

4. Tie the ends into a bow.

TRICK-OR-TREAT REFLECTIVE BAG
(brown paper bag, aluminum foil, yarn)

1. Fold over the top of a paper bag several times to make a cuff. Decorate the bag with jack-o'-lanterns cut from foil.

2. To make the braided handle, cut three pieces of yarn the same length. Line up the pieces, and tie them together into a knot about 1 inch from one end. Braid by folding A over B and then C over A. Continue until the yarn is braided. Tie the ends into a knot again about 1 inch from the end.

3. Staple the handle ends to the sides of the bag.

SPOOKY PICTURE
(construction paper, yarn)

1. Draw the outline of a spooky picture on a piece of construction paper.

2. Spread glue over one area of the picture at a time. Press strands of different-colored yarn into the glue.

RUB-A-DESIGN
(poster board, colored chalk, construction paper, paper towel, hair spray)

1. Draw and cut out a Halloween shape from a piece of poster board. On one side of the shape rub some colored chalk.

2. Place the shape with the chalk side faceup on the top of a folded sheet of construction paper.

3. With a small piece of paper towel, rub from the center of the chalky shape onto the paper. Lift the shape and see the design on the paper.

4. To keep the picture from smudging, spray it lightly with hair spray. Use the design to decorate a Halloween card.

JINGLE GHOSTS
(one-gallon plastic milk jug, thread, bells)

1. Wash and dry an empty one-gallon plastic milk jug. Cut ghost shapes from the sides of the jug.

2. Using a paper punch, make eye holes in each ghost. With a pen, punch a hole in the top of each ghost, and tie a thread loop for a hanger.

3. Poke a small hole with a pen at the bottom of each ghost. Place a small bell on a piece of thread, and tie it to the bottom of each ghost.

4. Hang the ghosts where the wind will make them flutter and the bells jingle.

HALLOWEEN PUZZLE
(plastic-foam tray, construction paper)

1. Cut a large square from the flat part of a plastic-foam tray.

2. Draw a picture on a piece of paper the same size as the plastic square. Glue the picture to the square.

3. When the picture is dry, cut through both the picture and the tray to make the puzzle pieces.

YARN-COVERED WITCH
(small box, orange yarn, black construction paper)

1. Cover the outside of the box with glue, except the bottom.

2. Press orange yarn into the glue to completely cover the top and sides of the box. Leave some yarn hanging down in loops at the bottom before starting back up the box, as shown.

3. For the hat brim, cut a circle of black construction paper. Cut another circle twice as big as the first one, and cut it in half.

4. Roll one of the halves into a cone shape, tape the ends together, and glue it to the brim.

5. Cut and glue on paper eyes and a mouth.

PAPIER-MÂCHÉ PUMPKIN
(flour and water, white paper towels, round balloon, poster paint, heavy cardboard, construction paper)

1. To make papier-mâché, mix flour and water together until it is the consistency of ketchup. Tear small strips of white paper towel and dip them into the flour mixture. Place a layer of strips on an inflated round balloon and let dry. Add another layer and let dry.

2. To make the pumpkin, cut a section from the bottom of the round papier-mâché shape so it will sit level and not roll away. Cover with poster paint and let dry.

3. To make the base, cut a rectangular piece of heavy cardboard. Cut various leaf shapes and glue on top. Glue the pumpkin to the center.

4. Add a paper stem, leaves, and vines to the pumpkin decoration.

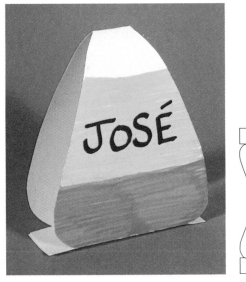

CORNY PLACE CARD
(white poster board)

1. On a piece of white poster board, draw and cut out the shape shown in the diagram.

2. Color the cutout to look like a giant piece of candy corn. Add a guest's name with a marker.

3. Fold as shown in the picture and glue together. Make one for each of your guests.

SCARY BLACK CAT
(poster board, cardboard egg carton, yarn, paper, brass fasteners)

1. Cut a large cat's head, body, and a tail from black poster board.

2. Cut three cup sections from a cardboard egg carton. Glue two in place for the eyes and one for the nose-mouth area. Add paper whiskers and a nose. Draw pupils on the eyes.

3. Attach a brass fastener at the neck and tail. Change the cat's position anytime you like.

SITTING WITCH
(cereal box, construction paper)

1. Cut a large corner from a cereal box. Cover it with black construction paper.

2. To make the hat brim, cut a circle from black paper. Cut a square hole in the center, and glue it over the point of the box corner.

3. Decorate with facial features, hands, legs, shoes, and a broom made from paper. Glue the legs to the inside edge at the front of the witch.

4. Set the witch on a shelf or on the edge of a desk.

TRICK-OR-TREAT BUCKET
(round plastic jug, brass fasteners, construction paper)

1. Soak the plastic jug in warm water to help soften it. Then cut away the top portion.

2. From the top portion, cut off a long strip about 1/2 inch wide for the handle.

3. Attach the handle to each side with a brass fastener.

4. Cut Halloween decorations from construction paper, and glue them around the bucket.

GHOSTLY GOGGLES
(construction paper)

1. Draw two ghost shapes, as shown, about the size of your hand. Cut out two circles in the body large enough to see through. Draw on faces with a marker.

2. Cut a 2-inch-wide headband long enough to go around your head.

3. Glue the ghosts' heads to the headband with the body hanging below so you can see through the holes. Tape the ends of the headband together.

ROCK CRAWLER
(small rock, poster paint, construction paper, cotton, chenille stick)

1. Cover a small rock with poster paint and let dry. Cut and glue pieces of construction paper for eyes.

2. Place a piece of cotton soaked in glue in the middle of the rock. (This keeps the legs from falling off when they are dry.)

3. Cut pieces of a chenille stick, and glue them across the cotton to make three legs on each side of the body. Let dry thoroughly.

4. Turn the stone over and slightly bend the chenille sticks at the ends so the "rocky crawler" can stand more easily.

WITCH FINGER-PUPPET
(construction paper, felt, yarn, self-adhesive stars)

1. Roll and glue together a wide piece of construction paper so your middle finger will fit inside it.

2. Decorate one side of the paper roll with pieces of felt and yarn.

3. Place self-adhesive stars on the witch's dress and hat.

ON-OFF PUMPKIN
(construction paper)

1. Fold a 1-foot strip of orange construction paper into three even sections. Trim the sides of the paper to form a pumpkin, but do not cut the folds.

2. Unfold the paper and cut out eyes, nose, and a mouth in the center section, making a pumpkin face.

3. Cover the top section with yellow construction paper and the bottom section with black.

4. Fold again, with the pumpkin facing you. Glue on a paper stem. Add lines with a marker or crayon to outline the pumpkin.

5. Fold so that the yellow paper shows through the pumpkin face when it is "on" and the black shows through when it is "off."

WITCH MOBILE
(brown paper bag, newspaper, paint, black crepe paper, yarn)

1. Paint a witch's face on the front of a paper bag. Stuff the bag with crumpled newspaper. Fold over the top and glue it shut.

2. For hair, glue strips of black crepe paper on the top of the bag. Attach a long piece of black yarn to the head with staples. Tie a knot in the yarn about 2 inches above the head.

3. Cut a circle of black paper for the brim of the hat. Make a hole in the center, and pull the yarn through, letting the brim rest on the knot.

4. To make the top of the hat, roll a piece of black paper in a cone shape. Thread the yarn through the top of the hat and tape the cone shape to the brim.

5. Glue yarn on the hat for a hatband.

CLOTHESPIN CRITTER
(two spring-type clothespins, construction paper, white paint)

1. From construction paper, cut four leg shapes long enough to cover a spring-type clothespin. Glue the legs on each side of two clothespins, with the feet at the open end.

2. On a piece of paper, draw shapes for the cat's body, tail, and head. Cut out the shapes, and glue them together. Add features with white paint.

3. Clip the clothespin legs to the cat's body. Position the legs so the cat will stand.

NOISY GOBLIN
(one-pint milk carton, dried beans, construction paper, yarn, ice-cream stick)

1. Place some dried beans inside a one-pint milk carton, then staple the top closed.

2. Spread glue on the carton, and cover it with construction paper.

3. Draw a scary face on one side. Staple on yarn at the top for hair.

4. Poke a small hole in the bottom of the carton, and glue an ice-cream stick in the hole for the handle.

PAPER OWL
(construction paper)

1. Fold a 3-inch-by-6-inch piece of construction paper in half lengthwise.

2. Starting on the fold, cut 1-inch slits—about 1/2 inch apart—the entire length of the paper. Open and glue the ends together to form the body.

3. Cut eyes, ears, and a beak from paper. Glue them in place.

4. Cut a strip of paper for a handle, and glue the ends to opposite sides of the owl body. Hang the owl on a branch or use it to decorate a table.

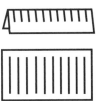

PUMPKIN PUPPET
(construction paper)

1. Cut two pieces of orange construction paper about 8 inches square. Staple them together on three sides with a stem at the top, as shown. Leave one side open.

2. To make the face, cut out and glue on eyes, a nose, and a mouth from paper.

3. Place your hand into the opened end to work the puppet. Make up spooky stories.

GLITTERY BRACELETS
(plastic or cardboard food containers, ribbon, aluminum foil, buttons, glitter, sequins)

1. From plastic or cardboard food containers, cut rings that will fit around your wrist as bracelets.

2. Decorate the rings with ribbon, aluminum foil, buttons, glitter, and sequins.

GHOST WIND SOCK

(sock, newspaper, ice-cream stick, black permanent marker)

1. Cut several slits in the leg section of an old white sock.

2. Wad up a sheet of newspaper, and stuff it into the foot of the sock. Place an ice-cream stick crosswise in the sock. Then stuff more newspaper in the sock to hold the ice-cream stick in place. Continue to stuff in more newspaper until you have filled the entire foot of the sock.

3. Make a face with a black permanent marker. With a pencil, poke two holes at the top of the ghost's head and pull a piece of yarn through them. Tie the ends together, and hang the ghost in a breezy place.

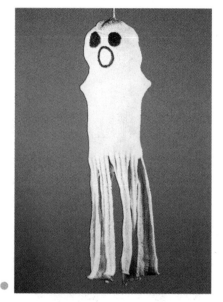

POMPON PUMPKIN

(lightweight cardboard, construction paper, orange yarn, poster board)

1. Cut out a pumpkin shape from a piece of lightweight cardboard, and cover it with orange construction paper.

2. To make pompons, wrap orange yarn around a piece of cardboard 4 inches square. (The more yarn you use, the fluffier the pompon will be.) Slip the yarn from the cardboard, and tie a piece of yarn tightly around the center, as shown. Cut through all the loops, and fluff up the yarn.

3. Glue the pompons on the pumpkin. Attach eyes, a nose, and a mouth made from black paper.

4. Attach the pompon pumpkin to a square piece of black poster board. Add a green paper stem. Glue a piece of yarn to the back for a hanger.

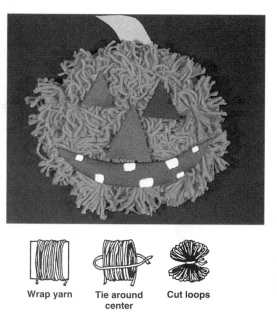

Wrap yarn   Tie around center   Cut loops

CAT NAPKIN HOLDER

(small cardboard tube, construction paper, napkin)

1. Cut a 1-inch section from a small cardboard tube. Cover it with black paper.

2. Draw a head, paws, and tail, as shown, on a piece of black construction paper and cut them out.

3. Decorate the head with features cut from paper. Glue the head, paws, and tail to the tube. Place a rolled napkin through the center.

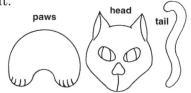

paws   head   tail

THE SPIDER AND THE WEB

(quart-size milk carton, yarn, construction paper, rickrack, cotton ball, paper cup, poster paint)

1. Measure 2 inches from the bottom of a quart-size milk carton, and draw a line around the outside of the carton. Cut along the line to make a small square box.

2. To create the web, poke eight holes around the sides of the box—one in each corner and one in the middle of each side. Tie a knot at one end of a long piece of yarn, and wrap a piece of tape around the other. Thread the taped end through the holes, as shown in the diagram, tying a knot in the yarn at the last hole. Take another piece of yarn, and loop it under and over the piece woven through the holes. Glue paper to the outside of the box and add rickrack.

3. For the body of the spider, dip a cotton ball into a small paper cup of water and poster paint. Squeeze the water out of the cotton ball and let dry. Separate a small piece of yarn into eight small strands. Glue the strands of yarn to the back of the cotton ball, letting the yarn hang down for legs. Add paper eyes and a mouth.

4. Glue the spider to the center of the web and wrap a few legs around the web.

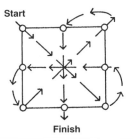

Start

Finish

HALLOWEEN POP-OUT CARD

(construction paper, plastic-foam tray)

1. For the card, fold a piece of construction paper in half. Fold it over in half again the other way.

2. Decorate the front of the card with cut pieces of paper. Write a greeting on another piece of paper, and glue it to the inside of the card.

3. Cut out a ghost from a plastic-foam tray and add paper eyes.

4. Cut two strips of paper and fold them over each other in the direction shown to form a paper spring. Glue the spring to the card and the back of the ghost.

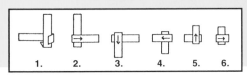

1. 2. 3. 4. 5. 6.

BOO TREAT BAG

(white paper, white paper bag)

1. Cut out two arms from white paper. Glue them to the sides of a white paper bag.

2. Draw a face on the front of the bag.

3. Fold down the top of the bag about an inch and trim the corners with scissors. Fill the bag with treats.

HANGING BATS
(construction paper, yarn)

1. Draw and cut out three pairs of bat designs from black construction paper. Divide into two sets. Set aside one of each bat design to use later.

2. Vertically lay the three bats of the first set on a table about 2 inches apart.

3. Cut a long piece of yarn, and lay it down the center of the bats. Glue the yarn to the bats.

4. Spread glue around the edges of the bats, and place the matching bat from the other set on top of its mate.

5. Tie a loop in the yarn above the first bat to make a hanger.

PUMPKIN CARD
(construction paper)

1. Cut a sheet of orange construction paper in half the long way. Fold in half again, as shown. Round off the corners into a pumpkin shape, being careful not to cut off the fold.

2. On the front, cut out the features. Cut a piece of black paper a little smaller than the folded card. Paste it behind the front of the card.

3. Write a message inside. Use the card as an invitation or greeting card.

GLITTERING WAND
(16-inch wooden dowel, poster paint, construction paper, felt, cotton balls, glitter)

1. For the handle, paint a wooden dowel and let it dry. Cut small stars from white construction paper, and glue them on the handle.

2. Cut two large identical stars from white felt. Spread glue on the edges of the stars.

3. Place a few cotton balls in the center of one star. Lay one end of the handle on top. Place the second star on top of the handle and the first star. Press the stars together at the edges.

4. Spread a thin layer of glue on one side of the star, and sprinkle with glitter. When it has dried, do the same to the other side.

PEBBLE PUMPKINS
(pebbles, paint, stick of wood)

1. To make pumpkins, wash and dry small round, flat pebbles. Paint them orange and create faces.

2. Use long, flat pebbles for the ghosts. Paint them white and create faces.

3. Glue the pumpkins and ghosts to a small stick of wood.

● ● ● ● ● ● ● ● ● ● ● ● ● ● ● ● ● ● ●

BEWITCHING EYES
(construction paper, brass fastener)

1. Glue together pieces of construction paper to create the witch's face, hair, and hat.

2. Cut two holes in the face for the eyes. Cut a small strip of paper and fold in the middle for the nose.

3. Draw and cut out a circle of white paper, no wider than the witch's face.

4. With the nose on top of the face and the circle behind the face, poke a brass fastener through the layers of paper to hold together.

5. Draw a pair of eyes on the white paper circle. Turn the circle and draw another set of eyes. Give your witch different eyes with each turn.

● ●

YARN HAIR WIG
(one knee-high stocking, large beverage container, yarn, crochet hook)

1. Pull a knee-high stocking, inside out, over your hair. Tie a knot close to your head in the extra stocking hanging loose. Take off the stocking and turn it right-side out. Stretch the stocking over a large beverage container.

2. Cut pieces of yarn 16 to 20 inches long. Hold a small pinch of stocking in your fingers. Gently poke a crochet hook through the stocking. Place a piece of yarn on the hook and pull it through the hole. Tie a knot in the yarn.

3. Continue to cover the stocking with pieces of yarn.

Special Costumes

BOX ROBOT
(a small and a large cardboard box, aluminum foil, construction paper, permanent markers)

1. To make the head, remove the flaps from a small cardboard box that fits on your shoulders. Cover the box with glue and aluminum foil. Cut out holes for the eyes and a mouth.

2. For the body, remove the flaps from a large cardboard box. Cut a hole in the bottom of the box for your head to fit through. Cut a square on each side of the box for your arms. Cover the box with glue and foil.

3. Decorate with construction paper and permanent markers. Twist together foil antennae, and tape them to the head.

CEREAL-BOX CLOWN
(family-sized cereal box, yarn, construction paper, tissue paper)

1. Cut off the back and the top sections of a family-sized cereal box. When placed on your head, it should almost touch your shoulders. Cover the box with glue and white paper. Cut out holes for eyes and a mouth. Cut and glue decorations from construction paper. Glue paper ears to the box sides.

2. Cut and glue loops of yarn to the box top to create hair. Make a hat by cutting out a paper circle. Make a slit to the center of the circle, pull the paper into a cone shape, and tape. Glue it on top of the hair.

3. Poke a hole in each side of the box behind the ears. Tie a piece of yarn from each hole to hold the mask on.

4. Make a collar by cutting a strip of paper long enough to go around your neck. Glue on gathered tissue paper and other decorations. Place the collar around your neck and tape in place.

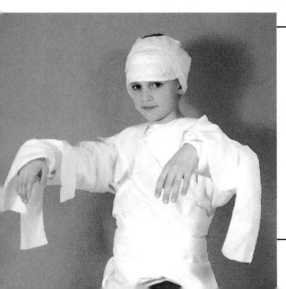

MUMMY
(old white sheet or fabric, white tape)

1. Wear a white or light-colored sweat suit. Cut strips from an old white sheet or other scrap fabric.

2. Tape one end of a strip to your clothes. Wrap the strip around your body, not too loose and not too tight. Tape the end of the strip to hold in place. Let some of the ends hang. Continue to wrap your body.

3. Wrap a strip around just the top of your head. Don't cover your face.

FLOWER
(poster board, yarn, tissue paper)

1. Cut three different petal sizes. Hold the petals together, and punch two holes so they will match from petal to petal.

2. To join together, work from left to right. Place a small petal on top of a large petal and thread a piece of yarn through the left holes of the petals. Place a medium petal between the large and small with the right hole of the large and small petals and the left hole of the medium petal lining up. Thread the yarn through the holes. Then place a large petal with its left hole, the medium petal with its right hole, and a small petal with its left hole lined up and thread the yarn through. Continue, then tie a knot at each end, leaving a piece of yarn to tie later.

3. For the center, cut a 2-inch strip of poster board, and staple to form a ring. Cut a tissue-paper circle larger than the ring. Glue it to the inside of the ring. Cut small circles of tissue paper. Place your finger in the middle of each circle and gather the paper around it. Glue the tip to the cap.

4. Tie the petals around your shoulders, and place the flower center on your head.

LION
(heavy paper plate, yarn, poster paint, felt)

1. To make the face, paint the outside bottom of a heavy paper plate. Draw and cut out holes for the eyes and a mouth. Decorate with yarn and a red-felt tongue.

2. To make the mane, cut pieces of yarn. With the lion's face down, glue the yarn on the rim of the paper plate.

3. Paper punch two holes close together on each side of the plate rim. Tie a piece of yarn to each hole to hold the mask in place.

BALLERINA
(seven chenille sticks, glitter)

1. Bend five 10-inch-long chenille sticks in half, then twist a 1/2-inch loop at the top. Lay the five pieces together in a row. Join them together, as shown. Make a loop at each bottom end. Attach these ends to a 3-inch-diameter ring made from a chenille stick.

2. For the top of the crown, bend one 12-inch chenille stick in half, twist a 1/2-inch loop at the top, and twist two extra side loops, as shown.

3. Make a loop at each bottom end. Fasten to the center of the crown. Dab glue over the crown, and sprinkle on glitter.

ASTRONAUT
(rectangular cardboard box, aluminum foil, large paper bag, fabric)

1. Tape or glue a piece of aluminum foil on one of the large sides of a rectangular cardboard box. Have an adult help you cut four slits, as shown. Slide a long strip of cloth through the slits and tie the ends so that the box can be worn as a backpack. Tape foil around the rest of the box.

2. To make a helmet, cut out a circle on one side of a paper bag for your face. Cut away about half of each side of the bag so that it fits over your shoulders. Cover the bag with foil using tape or glue. Cut the foil into pie-shaped wedges over the face hole and fold them inside.

3. Complete your costume by wearing boots and a pair of large gloves.

AUTOMOBILE
(corrugated cardboard box, poster paint, five large paper plates, small paper plates, fabric)

1. Open all the flaps on a corrugated cardboard box. Use poster paint to decorate sides of the cardboard to resemble a car.

2. Glue small paper plates to the front and back of the car to make headlights and tail lights. Glue four large paper plates to the car to make wheels. Staple a fifth large paper plate to the car to make a steering wheel.

3. Cut two long strips of fabric. Staple them to the top in the front and in the back of the car. Step into the car, and place the straps over your shoulders to carry the car.

RABBIT
(poster board, headband, paper clips, cotton balls, construction paper, large paper plate, yarn, elastic)

1. Fold a piece of white poster board in half. Cut out the ears, as shown. Place a headband inside the fold of each ear and glue them together, holding with paper clips until dry. Cover the headband and ears with glue and small cotton balls, adding pieces of pink construction paper.

2. Place a large paper plate in front of your face with the bottom facing out. Using a crayon, have a friend carefully mark on the outside of the plate where the eyeholes should be. Remove the plate and cut out the eyeholes.

3. Draw an outline around the eyes, and draw a nose and a mouth. Cut a tongue from paper. Glue on cotton balls, and add yarn whiskers. Staple elastic on opposite sides of the head to hold the mask in place.

4. Cover a round piece of poster board with cotton balls, and tape to the seat of your pants.

LADYBUG

(corrugated cardboard, poster board, black ribbon, paper towels, red tissue paper, mask)

1. Ask an adult to help cut a large oval, about the size of your back, from a piece of corrugated cardboard. Cover one side with red poster board, and cover the other side with black poster board. With an adult's help cut four slits, as shown. From the black side, insert a piece of black ribbon into each set of slits. Glue about 2 inches of the ribbon ends to the red side.

2. Cover the red side with crumpled paper towels glued in place to form a mound. Cover the mound with red tissue paper and glue at the edges. Cut and glue on yellow spots from poster board. Cut and staple six legs from black poster board.

PRINCE

(poster board, glitter, fabric, ribbon)

1. Draw a crown shape on a piece of poster board, as shown, and cut it out. Draw designs with glue and sprinkle them with glitter. Glue on ribbon and fabric pieces. Roll the cutout shape into the form of a crown. Leave the opening large enough to fit your head. Staple the ends together.

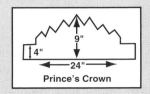

Prince's Crown

2. Cut a rectangular piece of fabric for a cape. Fold it in half, and cut a small section in the middle large enough for your head to go through.

3. Draw designs on the cape with glue and sprinkle them with glitter. Add ribbon and fabric pieces to match the crown. Let dry. Wear the cape over your clothes.

PRINCESS

(poster board, glitter, fabric, lace)

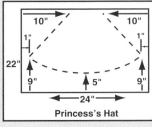

Princess's Hat

1. Draw a hat shape on a piece of poster board, as shown, and cut it out. Draw designs with glue and sprinkle them with glitter. Glue on ribbon and fabric pieces.

2. Roll the cutout into the shape of a cone to fit your head, and staple it in place. Leave a small opening at the top. Staple streamers of ribbons and fabric to the top of the hat. At the bottom, staple ribbon to hold the hat in place.

3. Follow step 2 and step 3 of the Prince costume to make a cape.

THREE-HEADED MONSTER
(four heavy cardboard paper plates, elastic, paint, paper, poster board)

1. To make the masks for your hands, cut one plate in half. Place one of the halves on a whole plate, face to face, and glue together at the rim. This forms a pocket for your hand. Repeat this for the second mask. To make the mask for your face, use one plate.

2. Punch holes at the top of each mask, and tie yarn for hair. Add other features with paint, paper, or poster board.

3. To wear the face mask, punch a hole on opposite sides of the plate, and tie a piece of elastic to each hole.

CHRISTMAS PACKAGE
(large cardboard box, gift wrap, small paper plate, ribbon)

1. Remove the top flaps from a large cardboard box so the top of the box will be open. Cut a hole in the bottom of the box large enough for your head to fit through.

2. Cut two holes on opposite sides of the box, large enough for your arms to fit through and for the box to rest on top of your shoulders. Decorate the box with gift wrap and ribbon.

3. Tape pieces of ribbon to the center of a small paper plate. Punch a hole on each side of the plate, and thread a piece of ribbon through the holes. Wear the plate on your head as the bow on top of the package.

LITTLE LEPRECHAUN
(poster board)

1. Cut hair and a beard from a piece of orange poster board. Draw a circle for your face in the middle and cut it out.

2. Draw and cut out a hat from green poster board. Glue the hat on top of the hair. Decorate the hat with a shamrock.

3. To make a pot of gold, cut out a large pot shape from a piece of black poster board. Cut small gold coins, and glue them around the top of the pot.

LADY AND GENTLEMAN
(old clothes and accessories)

1. Ask an adult to let you use some of his or her old clothes and accessories to play dress-up. Use your imagination to mix and match pieces of clothing, ties, hats, shoes, and old jewelry to make your own characters.

FIVE OF HEARTS
(four sheets of white poster board, red felt, red ribbon)

1. To make the front and back of a playing card, glue two sheets of white poster board together for one side of your body and two sheets together for the other side of your body.

2. To make the front side of the playing card, cut five large red-felt hearts, and glue them in place. Draw the numeral 5 in opposite corners of the card. Cut two small hearts from felt, and glue one below each number. Draw designs on the back side of the playing card.

3. Have someone help you hold up the card sections to the top of your shoulders, front and back. Cut strips of ribbon to fit over your shoulders, and staple them to the front and back of the card sections with the red hearts facing out for the front and the design facing out for the back.

4. Cut four strips of ribbon, and staple two of them to each side of the cards below your elbow. Tie the strips together in a bow to help hold the card in place on your body.

5. To make a hat, cut a long strip of poster board with a large heart in the middle. Cut out a red-felt heart, and glue it in the middle of the white one. Staple or tape the ends of the strips together to fit your head.

SURPRISE JACK-O'-LANTERN
(orange cellulose sponge, permanent marker, felt, chenille stick, flashlight)

1. Cut a pumpkin shape from a dry orange cellulose sponge (the kind that has irregular holes).

2. Draw lines on the pumpkin with a permanent marker. Cut out pieces of felt for the eyes, nose, and mouth, and glue them to the pumpkin.

3. Cut a small piece of chenille stick and loop it to form a stem. Glue it to the top of the pumpkin.

4. What's the surprise? Place a flashlight behind this jack-o'-lantern, and watch it glow in the dark!

TRICK-OR-TREAT TOTE
(large cereal box, half-gallon milk carton, construction paper, yarn)

1. Cut off the two long top flaps of a large cereal box. Fold back and glue the two small top flaps to each narrow side of the outside of the cereal box. These will be reinforcements for the handle.

2. Cut a half-gallon milk carton in half. Cover the milk carton and the cereal box with glue and black construction paper. Glue them together.

3. Draw and cut out ghost shapes from paper and glue them to the tote-box. Add yarn around the top edges.

4. Poke a small hole on each narrow side of the cereal box. Thread the ends of a piece of yarn through the holes from the outside of the box, and tie the yarn into knots on the inside of the box.

HALLOWEEN BANNER
(paper)

1. To create the word "HAPPY," you will need a piece of paper that measures 5 by 15 inches. You may need to tape pieces of paper together.

2. Starting at the narrow end, fold over 3 inches of the paper and continue to fold into accordion pleats until the whole piece is pleated.

3. With a pencil, lightly sketch a ghost, as shown in the diagram, on the top of the folded paper. Cut around the ghost shape, but don't cut on the folds. You should have five ghosts. Write one letter of the word "HAPPY" on each ghost.

4. To create the word "HALLOWEEN," follow steps 1, 2, and 3, using a piece of paper measuring 5 by 27 inches.

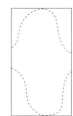

POP-OUT GHOST

(plastic container with snap-on lid, construction paper,
small plastic-foam ball, tissue paper, thread)

1. Cover a plastic container with strips of gray construction paper. Cover the snap-on lid with a circle of paper. With a marker, draw stones on the paper.

2. Cut two strips of paper 1 inch wide. Fold the strips over each other, as shown in the diagram on page 27, to form a long spring. The spring, when flattened, should be the height of the can. Glue one end of it to the inside bottom of the container.

3. Cover a small plastic-foam ball with white tissue, and secure with thread at the neck. Add eyes and a mouth to the ghost. Spread out the ghost body and glue the bottom of the ball to the other end of the spring.

4. Push the ghost inside the container and close the lid. Surprise a friend by opening the lid. See the ghost pop up and down.

GOBLIN CUP

(plastic-foam cup, construction paper)

1. Tape or glue construction paper to the outside of a plastic-foam cup.

2. Add features such as ears, eyes, a mouth, and a nose from paper to create your goblin.

SPIDER HAT

(paper plates, yarn, chenille sticks, 2 1/2-inch plastic-foam ball, paper)

1. Cut the center from one paper plate without cutting through the rim. Cut another paper plate, from the edge to the center. Staple this plate into a cone shape.

2. Glue the cone to the rim. Use a paper punch to punch a hole on each side of the hat, and add yarn for ties.

3. Draw a spider web on the cone. Spread glue and pieces of yarn over the web. Color a 2 1/2-inch plastic-foam ball with a marker. Push chenille sticks into the ball for legs. Add paper eyes.

4. Glue the spider to the top of the hat, attaching his legs somewhere on the web.

PAPER-PLATE PUMPKIN
(two 9-inch paper plates, construction paper, string, poster paint)

1. Glue two 9-inch paper plates right sides together. Place a green stem cut from construction paper and a piece of string in between the plates at the top before the glue dries.

2. Paint the plates orange and let dry.

3. To make the face, cut features from paper, and glue them onto the front of the pumpkin.

HAPPY HALLOWEEN BASKET
(plastic food containers, bathroom tissue tube, paint, paper, self-adhesive stars)

1. Paint a happy face on an upright bathroom tissue tube and let it dry. Cut a strip of paper, decorate it, and glue each end to the inside of the tube for a handle.

2. Glue the tube in the center of a plastic margarine container. Add self-adhesive stars around the outside.

3. Fill the basket with treats.

DANCING GOBLIN
(cardboard egg carton, poster paint, yarn, construction paper, two marbles)

1. Cut four identical cup sections from a cardboard egg carton.

2. To make the head, glue two of the cups together and let dry. Cover with paint and let dry again. Cut eyes, a nose, and a mouth from construction paper, and glue them to the cup for the face. Glue short pieces of thin yarn to the top of the head for hair.

3. To make the feet, poke a hole in each of the two remaining cups. Paint the cups and let them dry. Cut two pieces of thick yarn about 7 inches long, and thread one piece into each hole. Tie a knot at the ends so the yarn won't come out of the cups.

4. Attach the feet to the head by poking a hole on each side of the head and gluing the ends of the yarn into these holes.

5. Glue a marble inside each foot for weight. Hold the goblin with your fingers, and tilt his head back and forth quickly to make him dance.

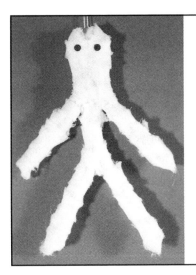

WOODEN-STICK MUMMY
(five ice-cream sticks, gauze, paper, string)

1. Glue five ice-cream sticks together, as shown, to make the body.

2. Cut a head shape from paper and glue it to the body.

3. Cut strips of gauze. Spread some glue along the sticks and head and wrap the gauze around them.

4. With a paper punch, punch out two paper eyes and glue them to the head. Glue a string loop to the back of the mummy for a hanger.

Body

GHOSTLY GAME
(shoe box and lid, poster paint, large thread spool, white paper, three Ping-Pong balls)

1. Remove the lid from an empty shoe box. Paint the inside of the lid with black poster paint and let dry. Paint three Ping-Pong balls black and let dry.

2. Draw a ghost shape on a piece of white paper to fit the inside of the lid. Cut out the ghost and glue it inside the lid.

3. To make the eyes and mouth, place a large thread spool on the face and trace around the spool. Cut out along the outline. Turn the shoe box upside down, and hold the lid against the bottom. Trace around the holes for the eyes and mouth, then cut along the outlines.

4. Glue the lid to the bottom of the box, matching the holes. Cut out sections of the sides of the shoe box to make legs.

5. Drop the three balls onto the lid. Hold the box in your hands, and roll the balls around until you have filled the holes.

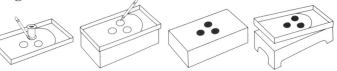

FUZZY SPIDERS
(four black chenille sticks, one large four-hole button, construction paper)

1. Cut four black chenille sticks about 6 inches in length.

2. Push a chenille stick through each hole of a large four-hole button. Bend and shape the sticks to look like legs.

3. To make the spider's head and body section, cut a piece of black construction paper. Glue it to the top of the button. Add paper eyes.

GHOSTLY HAND PUPPET
(white paper, yarn, black crayon)

1. Cut two identical ghost shapes, larger than your hand, from white paper.

2. Hold one ghost on top of the other. With a paper punch, punch holes around the sides and tops.

3. Cut a long piece of yarn. Lace the front and back together by going in and out of the holes. Tie a knot in the ends of the yarn.

4. Draw a ghost face with black crayon. Place your hand in the puppet, and say "Boo!"

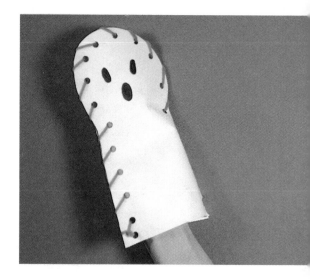

FUNNY-FACE PUMPKIN
(construction paper)

1. Cut out three identical paper pumpkin shapes with straight bottoms.

2. Fold each pumpkin in half and then open up. Draw a different face on each paper pumpkin, using the fold as a guide to center the face.

3. Add glue to one half of the back of two pumpkins, and glue these together. Then glue the third pumpkin to the remaining back sections.

TREAT BAGS
(small white paper bags, construction paper)

1. Decorate one side of a small white paper bag with cutout pieces of construction paper. Glue them in place.

2. Make Halloween cats, witches, goblins, or other creatures. Let your imagination loose.

3. Place treats inside each bag for your friends.

HALLOWEEN HOUSE
(construction paper)

1. Fold a square piece of paper into sixteen squares, as shown in the diagram. Cut on the solid lines (Fig.1).

2. Fold B over C and staple (Fig. 2). Fold F over G and staple.

3. Bring A and D together, overlapping slightly, and staple (Fig. 3). Do the same with E and H.

4. Draw doors and windows, and decorate the house as you wish.

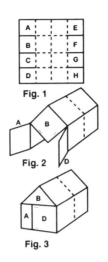

Fig. 1

Fig. 2

Fig. 3

THREE-D CAT
(heavy cardboard, poster paint)

1. From heavy cardboard, cut out the body, front legs, back legs, and head. Make slits in these four parts, as shown.

2. Slide the legs and head into the body slits to be sure that the parts fit properly. Take apart.

3. Paint the parts with poster paint, adding features. Let dry, then put the parts back together.

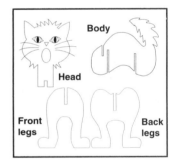

TONGUE DEPRESSOR FINGER PUPPETS
(permanent markers, watercolor or tempera paint, tongue depressors, felt, lightweight cardboard)

1. Paint a face on a tongue depressor with permanent marker, watercolor, or tempera paint. Features can be added with pieces of felt.

2. Glue a lightweight piece of cardboard in the shape of a ring to the back of each tongue depressor. When dry, place the puppets on your fingers.

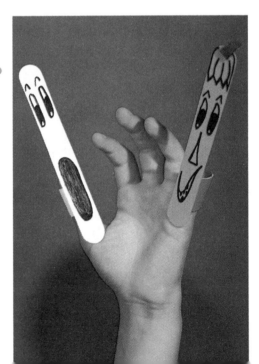

OWL NAPKIN HOLDER
(bathroom tissue tube, poster paint, construction paper)

1. Draw two V shapes, one at each end of a bathroom tissue tube, and cut them out. Glue the V shapes to each side of the tube for ears.

2. Paint the tube and let dry. Cut out eyes and a beak from paper and glue in place.

3. Place a rolled napkin inside the tube and stand the owl up.

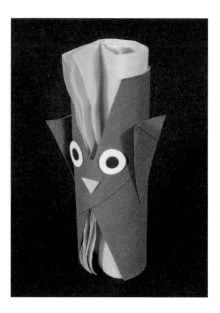

• •

TRICK-OR-TREAT FUN BOX
(small cardboard gift box, construction paper, poster board)

1. Cover the lid of a small cardboard gift box with construction paper. Tape the ends inside the lid.

2. Cut the face of a witch from white paper, and glue it to the top of the lid. Draw on facial features with a marker.

3. Cut a poster board hat, and glue it to the witch. Fill the box with treats for a friend.

• • • • • • • • • • • • • • • **EERIE HOUSE CARD** • • • • • • • • • • • • • • •
(construction paper)

1. Fold a piece of dark blue construction paper in half for the card. On the outside write this message: "Dear _____, On Halloween will you help me haunt a house? Look inside."

2. On black construction paper, draw a house that will fit inside the card. Add windows and a door with a marker or a crayon. Cut out the house.

3. From white paper, cut out a ghost shape longer than the height of the house. On the bottom of the ghost print "PUSH UP."

4. Inside the card, put the house in place with the ghost behind it. Put glue on the back of the house but only at the sides. Be sure the ghost moves freely.

5. Pull the ghost down so that it is invisible until your friend follows the instruction "PUSH UP."

GOBLIN TREE
(cream containers, construction paper, tree branch,
plastic food container, modeling clay, fabric, yarn, string)

1. For each goblin, glue together two small cream containers. Cut features from paper to decorate each goblin.

2. Stick a fallen tree branch into a plastic food container filled with modeling clay. Cut a circle of fabric. Wrap it around the container and tie it together with yarn.

3. Glue a piece of string to the top of each goblin, and tie the goblins to the branches.

BLACK CAT MOBILE
(plastic food container, yarn, cardboard egg carton, poster paint, construction paper)

1. For the top section, cut a ring from a plastic food container. Punch four evenly spaced holes near the top of the ring. Insert a piece of yarn through each hole, tying a knot at the end. Gather the four pieces at the top, and tie them together into one knot.

2. Cut out five egg-carton sections and make them into the shapes of cats' heads, as shown. Paint them black. Add whiskers and eyes with paper and glue. Poke a hole in the top of each cat's head.

3. On the bottom of the ring, punch five evenly spaced holes. Thread a piece of yarn through each cat's head and through a hole in the ring. Tie a knot at each end.

4. Glue a piece of black paper to cover the back of each head. Add paper ears.

PUMPKIN PIN
(frozen-juice pull-top lid, felt, safety pin)

1. Place a frozen-juice pull-top lid on a piece of felt, and trace around it with a pencil. Do this again and cut out the two circles.

2. Glue one felt circle to each side of the lid.

3. Cut out a mouth, a nose, eyes, and a stem from pieces of felt, and glue them in place.

4. On the other side, glue or tape a safety pin.

BAT ERASER
(pencil, rubber eraser cap, permanent marker, construction paper)

1. Place a rubber eraser cap on the top of a pencil. With scissors, cut out a small notch at the top of the eraser to form two pointed ears.

2. Color the eraser black with a permanent marker.

3. Cut out bat wings from construction paper. Glue the wings to the back of the eraser and let dry. Cut out small paper eyes, and glue them to the bat.

FLASHY JACK-O'-LANTERN
(brown paper bag, flashlight)

1. Place a brown paper bag on a table, with the open end at the bottom.

2. Draw and cut out a pumpkin face on the bag.

3. At night, place the bag over a small flashlight. See the pumpkin glow in the dark!

SCARECROW
(one medium and one small brown paper bag, newspaper, straw hat, construction paper)

1. For the body, use a medium-size brown paper bag. For the arms, roll a few sheets of newspaper into a tube. Poke a hole in each side of the bag near the top, and push the arms through. Stuff the body with crumpled newspaper, fold the opening closed, and staple it shut.

2. For the head, use a small paper bag stuffed with newspaper. Twist and tape the bag shut. Make a small hole in the body and insert the twisted end of the head into the hole. Use tape to hold it in place.

3. Roll a few sheets of newspaper into two small tubes for the legs. Poke two holes in the bottom of the body and insert the legs. Add tape to hold them in place.

4. Glue on cut paper for features and patches. Cut and glue paper hay for the feet, hands, neck, and head. Add an old straw hat.

GHOSTLY GREETINGS
(black construction paper, white crayon, white plastic bread wrapper)

1. Fold a piece of black construction paper into quarters to make a card.

2. Use white crayon to draw the outline of a ghost on the front of the card. Open the card and cut the ghost outline out of the card.

3. Tape a piece of white plastic cut from a bread wrapper behind the cutout ghost so that when the card is refolded the white plastic shows through the front of the card. Cut black paper dot eyes and a mouth and glue to the ghost.

4. On the front of the card, use white crayon to write "Boo!" On the inside of the card, write a message and your name.

SPIN-A-WEB BRACELET
(wide plastic ribbon holder, felt, yarn, sequins, heavy black thread on a spool)

1. Glue a piece of white felt around a wide plastic ribbon holder.

2. Cut the body of a spider from felt. Glue on yarn legs. Add sequins for eyes. Glue the spider on the white felt.

3. Tape the end of heavy black thread to the inside of the holder. Holding the spool of thread in your hand, wrap thread around the inside and outside of the holder to look like a spider's web. Cut the thread and tape the end.

COLONIAL WIG
(brown paper bag, cotton balls, ribbon)

1. Find a brown paper bag that will fit on your head.

2. Cut the bag in the shape of a wig, as shown. Cut out a ponytail from the leftover paper, and glue it to the back of the wig.

3. Spread some glue over a section of the wig, and press cotton balls into it until the wig and ponytail are covered.

4. Tie a piece of ribbon around the ponytail and make a bow.

EGG-CARTON WITCH
(cardboard egg carton, construction paper, yarn)

1. For the witch's head, cut four adjoining sections from a cardboard egg carton.

2. Using the inside of the carton as the face, glue on eyes, a mouth, and a wart. Add a black construction-paper hat to the back of the cardboard egg carton.

3. Glue long pieces of black yarn over the top of the witch's head, letting it hang down around her face.

4. Add a yarn hanger to the back of the witch.

GHOST-IN-A-BOX
(cotton balls, facial tissue, rubber band, metal bandage box, paper)

1. To make the ghost, center two or three cotton balls in two facial tissues. Place a small rubber band around the bottom of the tissue ball to form the ghost's neck. Draw a face with a marker.

2. Place the ghost's body into a metal bandage box. Tape the back of the ghost's head to the inside lid of the box. Close the lid gently, tucking the head into the box.

3. Decorate the outside of the metal bandage box with paper to give the ghost a home. Pull open the lid and the ghost will pop up.

OWL TREE
(plastic food container, tree branch, clay, small stones, paper, hemlock pinecones, plastic food wrap)

1. Place a fallen tree branch into a plastic food container filled with small stones and clay. Decorate the outside with paper.

2. To make owls, decorate the hemlock pinecones with paper eyes and beaks.

3. Glue the owls to the fallen tree branch. To help hold them in place, wrap a small piece of plastic food wrap around them. Remove the wrap when almost dry.

JUMPING CRITTER
(cardboard egg carton, dried beans, poster paint, paper, elastic, button)

1. For the body, cut two egg cups from a cardboard egg carton. Glue the two cups together with a few dried beans inside.

2. Paint the body with poster paint and let dry. Add eyes, a nose, a mouth, and hair from pieces of paper.

3. Glue a long piece of elastic to the top. Thread the other end through the holes of a button and tie a knot. Slip the button between your fingers and make the critter jump.

HALLOWEEN CAT
(construction paper)

1. Cut a piece of black construction paper about 5 inches by 8 inches. Measure 2 inches down on the long side and draw a line across the paper.

2. In the center above the 2-inch line, draw the head of a cat. Cut along the line and the outline of the cat. Roll the paper cat into a tube and tape the edges together.

3. Cut and glue on eyes, a nose, a mouth, and whiskers. Cut claws and two paws from paper and tape them to the bottom of the paper tube.

4. For the tail, glue the ends of two long, narrow strips of paper together at a right angle, as shown. Then fold one strip across the other alternately, as shown by the arrows.

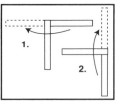

Continue until almost at the end, then cut tiny strips for fringe. Glue the other end to the cat.

PUMPKIN BOOKMARK
(construction paper)

1. Cut a long stem from green construction paper.

2. Cut small orange pumpkins, and glue them on the stem.

3. On a pumpkin, write the name of a book you have read during the Halloween season. Add a book title to each pumpkin after you have read other books.

Papier-Mâché Masks

These masks are created with papier-mâché. Simply mix flour and water together until it is the consistency of ketchup. Tear strips of newspaper or paper towel and dip them into the mixture. Pull them through your fingers to remove excess mixture. Layer the strips to create the mask. Allow a day or two for the papier-mâché to dry before painting.

CAT

(large heavy paper plate, lightweight cardboard, papier-mâché, poster paint, elastic)

1. Facing the outside bottom of a large heavy paper plate, trim the plate to form the cat's head. Cut ears from lightweight cardboard and staple in place. Cover with papier-mâché.

2. To make the nose and cheeks, cover small wads of paper with papier-mâché. Add a small papier-mâché tongue. Let dry.

3. Add features with poster paint. Cut out eyeholes, and staple elastic to opposite sides of the mask to fit around your head.

SUN

(large heavy paper plate, lightweight cardboard, papier-mâché, poster paint, elastic)

1. Use the outside bottom of a large heavy paper plate for the sun. To make rays, cut triangular pieces from lightweight cardboard, and staple them around the sun.

2. Cover the entire sun with papier-mâché, adding rolled pieces of papier-mâché to create eyebrows and a mouth. Let dry.

3. Paint with poster paint and let dry. Cut out eyeholes. Staple a piece of elastic to opposite sides of the mask to fit around your head.

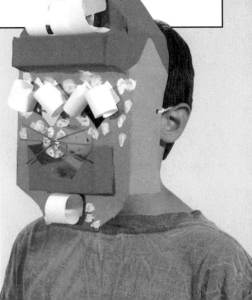

ALIEN

(cardboard cereal box, small boxes, thread spool, papier-mâché, poster paint, toothpicks, paper, elastic)

1. Remove the back and bottom sections from a cardboard cereal box. Tape the top flaps closed. Tape on small boxes to form features. Add a thread spool for a nose. Cover with papier-mâché and let dry.

2. Paint with poster paint. Add toothpicks to the nose and curled pieces of paper for hair. Cut out eyeholes, and staple a piece of elastic to opposite sides of the mask to fit around your head.

BEAR
(large heavy paper plate, lightweight cardboard, small heavy paper bowl, papier-mâché, poster paint, elastic)

1. To make the snout of the bear, turn over a small heavy paper bowl, and place on top of the outside bottom of a large heavy paper plate. Tape it on the plate. Cut small ears from pieces of lightweight cardboard, and staple them to the plate.

2. Cover with papier-mâché, adding rolled pieces of papier-mâché to form the eyebrows. Let dry.

3. Paint and let dry. Add features with poster paint. Let dry. Cut out eyeholes. Staple a piece of elastic to opposite sides of the mask to fit around your head.

WITCH
(cardboard candy box, papier-mâché, poster paint, elastic)

1. Use the outside of a cardboard candy box with a lid to create the witch. Cut and tape together, as shown.

2. Cover the box and lid with papier-mâché. To make the nose, cover a wad of paper with papier-mâché. Add strips of papier-mâché to create eyebrows and a mouth. Fold a strip of papier-mâché for cheeks.

3. Paint the features with poster paint and let dry. Cut out eyeholes. Staple a piece of elastic to opposite sides of the mask to fit around your head.

Cut hat shape
Cut lid
Cut lid
Tape lid box

MOUSE
(large heavy paper plate, three small paper plates, papier-mâché, poster paint, elastic)

1. Use the outside bottom of a large heavy paper plate for the face of the mouse. To make ears, staple two small paper plates, right-side up, to the large plate.

2. To make the nose, cut a small section from a small paper plate, as shown. Bend it to form the point of a nose, and tape it in place on the face. Cover the nose, ears, and face with papier-mâché and let dry.

Cut on dotted line.

3. Decorate with poster paint, adding features, and let dry. Cut out eyeholes. Staple a piece of elastic to opposite sides of the mask to fit around your head.

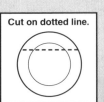

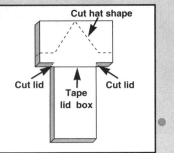

FLYING BAT
(black poster board, black elastic, heavy black thread)

1. Fold a large piece of black poster board in half.

2. With the board folded, draw and cut out half a bat shape.

3. Staple the end of a piece of black elastic, like the kind used on masks, to each wing. Tie a piece of heavy black thread to the middle of the elastic.

4. Bounce the bat to make it "fly."

BIG EYES
(7-inch paper plates, construction paper, frame from an old pair of plastic eyeglasses)

1. Glue and tape two 7-inch paper plates together, side by side. Cut large eyes and eyelids from construction paper, and glue them in place.

2. Hold the paper-plate eyes up to your face and have an adult help mark a place for your eyes. Remove from your face. Cut or punch eyeholes on the marks.

3. Tape a frame from an old pair of plastic eyeglasses to the back of the big eyes so they will be easy to wear.

PARTY HAT
(10-inch heavy paper plate, poster paint, yarn)

1. Cut from the edge to the center of a 10-inch heavy paper plate. Pull one cut edge over the other to form a cone-shaped hat. Staple in place.

2. Paint Halloween decorations on the hat and let dry.

3. Cut twenty to thirty short pieces of yarn. Tie together in the center. Glue to the top of the hat for a pompon.

4. Punch one hole on opposite sides of the base of the hat, and attach a piece of yarn for a tie.

HALLOWEEN CANDY HOLDER
(round cardboard food container with plastic lid, aluminum foil, construction paper, small aluminum pie tin, brass fastener, chenille stick)

1. Remove the plastic lid from a round cardboard food container. Cover the container with aluminum foil. Decorate it with pieces of construction paper.

2. Using a brass fastener, attach the center of a small aluminum pie tin to the center of the plastic lid.

3. To make a flower, cut circles of different-colored paper. Hold them together and punch two holes in the center, like a button. Thread a chenille stick through the holes, and twist in the back to make a stem.

4. Punch two holes in the side of the aluminum pie tin, and fasten the stem of the flower.

5. Fill the cardboard container with candy. Put some candy in the aluminum pie tin, and place the lid on top of the container.

HALLOWEEN GOURD
(small gourd, construction paper, yarn, pompon)

1. Wash and dry a small gourd. Cut and glue on pieces of construction paper to create a face on the lower half.

2. Spread a line of glue around the gourd above the face. Cut small pieces of black yarn. Press the yarn into the glue to create hair.

3. Glue a black pompon at the tip of the gourd. Add a loop of yarn for a hanger.

SPIDER CARD
(white poster board, black yarn, construction paper)

1. Fold a 6-by-8-inch piece of white poster board in half to make a card. With the fold at the top, find the center of the front of the card. Draw a circle, 1 1/2 inches in diameter, and cut it out.

2. With the card still folded, draw around the circle, making an outline on the inside of the card.

3. Open the card. Spread glue in the circle, and cover it with yarn by going around in a spiral until the circle is covered. This is the spider's body.

4. Add eight legs to the body using pieces of yarn. Add a paper head and eyes. Write "HAPPY HALLOWEEN." Close the card, and all you will see is the spider's body.

SPOOKY PLACE CARD
(paper, permanent marker, pennies, drinking straw)

1. Draw and cut out a ghost shape from paper. Draw eyes and a mouth. Outline the edges of the ghost with a permanent marker. Punch a hole in the mouth of the ghost.

2. Glue a penny under each "hand."

3. Put the straw through the ghost's mouth, letting the body of the ghost rest on the rim of the glass.

HALLOWEEN PLACE MAT
(white poster board, clear self-adhesive paper)

1. Cut a large rectangle from a piece of white poster board. With markers, draw a Halloween scene.

2. Have an adult help you cover your scene with clear self-adhesive paper. Fold the extra paper to the back of the board or trim at the edges.

3. Reuse your place mat by cleaning it with a damp cloth.

WITCH PIN
(cardboard, yellow and black felt, dried grass, sequin, safety pin)

1. Cut out two 2 1/2-inch circles, one from lightweight cardboard and one from black felt. Glue them together.

2. Cut a slightly smaller circle from yellow felt and glue it to the center of the black circle.

3. From black felt, draw and cut out a witch that will fit on the yellow felt circle.

4. Use pieces of dried grass to make a broom and glue it to the yellow circle. Glue the witch on top of the broom.

5. Add a sequin eye. Glue a small safety pin to the back.

TUBE GHOST FAMILY
(corrugated cardboard, paper, paper towel tubes, facial tissue)

1. To make the base, cut out a piece of corrugated cardboard. Trace around the shape on a piece of black paper and cut it out. Glue the paper on top of the cardboard.

2. For each body, cut a paper towel tube in a different length. Glue or tape white paper around each tube.

3. For each head, roll facial tissue into a small ball. Place two facial tissues over the ball as smoothly as possible, and tape together at the bottom of the ball.

4. Glue the heads to the bodies. Add black paper eyes and mouths.

BLACK-BEAN CAT
(poster board, black beans, kidney beans, pumpkin seeds, dried green peas, broom straw, yarn)

1. Draw and cut out a cat shape from black poster board. Glue black beans on it for the body.

2. Add pumpkin seeds and dried green peas for eyes. Use a pumpkin seed for a nose and two kidney beans for the mouth. Cut small pieces of broom straw for whiskers.

3. After all the seeds and beans have dried, glue the cat on a large piece of orange poster board. Add a yarn hanger to the back.

BONE NECKLACE
(2 cups flour, 1 cup salt, 1 cup cold water, bowl, spoon, waxed paper, plastic drinking straw, cookie tray, oven mits, shoestring)

1. In a bowl, stir together the flour, salt, and water. Knead, or work the mixture together with your hands, until it forms a smooth dough.

2. Place a small amount of flour on a piece of waxed paper. Roll some of the dough into small balls. Press to flatten them slightly. Use a plastic drinking straw to poke a hole in the center of each shape. Shape larger dough pieces, poking holes in some of them.

3. Have an adult help you dry the dough pieces in a 325°F oven for one to two hours or until they feel hard to the touch. Remove from the tray, and place them on a wire rack to cool.

4. Tie a large-shaped bone in the middle of the shoestring, and string smaller ones on each side of it. Tie a bow at the ends.

SCARECROW PUPPET
(three plastic drinking straws, tongue depressor, felt, straw)

1. Cut three plastic drinking straws in half. Glue three pieces to a tongue depressor vertically for the body and three horizontally for the arms. Leave space at the top of the tongue depressor for a head and space at the bottom for feet.

2. Fold a piece of felt in half, and cut out a coat shape. Cut a small slit in the fold for a neck opening, and slip the coat over the head of the body. Glue the coat in place, stuffing a few pieces of straw at the hands and feet. Add felt buttons.

3. Cut a felt hat and a round piece of felt for the head. Glue in place. Add a few pieces of straw, and draw on a face with a marker.

CREPE-PAPER BUG
(crepe paper, thread, poster board, sequins)

1. Wrap a 1 3/4-by-6-inch piece of crepe paper around a pencil, and glue in place. Let dry.

2. Push the ends of the paper toward the center of the pencil to crush. Remove the pencil. At one end, tie off a head section with thread. Stuff a small ball of crepe paper in this part for the head, and glue to close.

3. Cut a strip of poster board as long as the bug from neck to tail. Cut legs from both sides of the strip and bend down. Glue the body to the legs.

4. Add sequins to the body and to the head for eyes.

TUBE SURPRISE
(bathroom tissue tube, tissue paper, yarn, paper)

1. Place some wrapped candies inside a bathroom tissue tube.

2. Cut a piece of orange tissue paper so it will measure at least 3 inches beyond each tube end.

3. Wrap the tissue paper around the tube, and close the ends with pieces of yarn.

4. Cut a bone shape from paper, and glue on the tube.

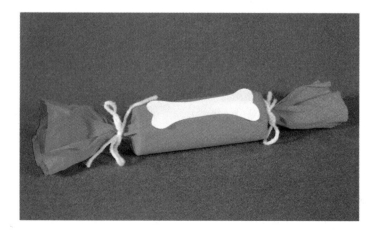

HOLIDAY PLATE COVER
(two heavy paper plates, poster paint, cotton balls, construction paper, moveable plastic eyes)

1. Paint the outside of one heavy paper plate with poster paint and let dry.

2. Glue cotton balls on top to make ghosts. Add moveable plastic eyes.

3. Cut pieces of construction paper to make pumpkins with cutout faces and leaves.

4. Place cookies or other treats on the undecorated paper plate. Use the decorated plate to cover the treats.

PUMPKIN-SEED BOX
(small cardboard jewelry box, pumpkin seeds, clear nail polish)

1. Glue pumpkin seeds around the outer edge of the box lid to form a design. Glue seeds to the top of the box lid, again forming a design.

2. After the seeds have dried, cover them with a coat of clear nail polish to give them a nice shine.

PUMPKIN TREAT HOLDER
(small cardboard food container with lid, construction paper, chenille stick)

1. Glue orange construction paper to the outside of a small cardboard food container and its lid. Cut out paper features for a jack-o'-lantern face, and glue them to the container.

2. Add a green leaf to the middle of the lid. Punch two holes in the lid, making it look like a button, and insert a chenille stick. Twist it together to form a stem.

3. Store treats inside the holder.

BLACK-CAT STICK PUPPET
(ice-cream stick, construction paper, yarn)

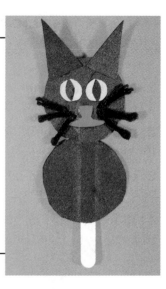

1. Cut four identical circles from black construction paper. Glue two circles to one side of an ice-cream stick and two to the other side to form the body and head of the cat.

2. Cut ears, eyes, and a mouth from paper, and glue to the head.

3. Glue pieces of black yarn to the face to make whiskers, and add a piece to the back of the cat for a tail.

WITCH'S HAT
(black poster board)

1. Draw a large circle about 14 to 18 inches in diameter on a piece of large black poster board. Draw a circle in the center about 5 to 8 inches in diameter. (The size really depends on how large your head is.)

2. Cut out the small center circle. Cut tabs along the inside edge, as shown.

3. Draw another circle about 9 to 12 inches in diameter on black poster board. Cut a section from the circle, as shown in the diagram. Roll the section into a cone shape, fitting it over the tabs of the brim.

4. Use transparent tape to hold the cone shape together. Tape the tabs to the inside of the cone.

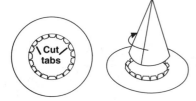

JACK-O'-LANTERN SPECTACLES
(poster board, chenille sticks)

1. For the lenses of the spectacles, cut two circles from a piece of orange poster board. Draw two off-center circles on the lenses for the eyes, and cut them out.

2. Draw black triangle-shaped eyes, a nose, and a big smiling mouth in the area next to each eyehole.

3. Cut a small piece of chenille stick, and glue it to the lenses to make the nosepiece.

4. For the earpieces, punch a hole on opposite sides of the spectacles. Insert a chenille stick into each hole. Twist the ends together. Be sure they are long enough to fit comfortably over your ears.

GHOST STATIONERY
(potato, table knife, black construction paper, white paint, white crayon)

1. Wash and dry a potato. Cut the potato in half. Trace around the potato half, with the cut-side down, on a piece of paper. Cut it out. Draw a ghost on the potato tracing and cut it out.

2. Place the ghost pattern on the cut-side of the potato. Have an adult help you use the table knife to cut away the area around the ghost, leaving it about 1/2 inch higher than the rest of the potato.

3. Paint the ghost design with white paint, and press it onto a piece of black construction paper. Repeat the painting and printing until you have the design you want. Let dry.

4. Write a message with a white crayon.

PUMPKIN DECORATION
(two heavy paper plates, poster paint, tissue paper, felt, plastic-foam tray)

1. Draw eyes, a nose, and a mouth, making a pumpkin face on one heavy paper plate. Cut them out. Place the paper plate on top of the second plate, trace around the openings, and cut them out.

2. Paint the outside of each plate orange, and glue a piece of yellow tissue over the facial features on the inside of the plates. Glue the plates together, rim to rim with the painted sides facing out.

3. Make a slot in a green plastic-foam tray. Stand the pumpkin in the tray. Add glue and let dry.

4. Add a felt stem to the top of the pumpkin, and glue leaves around the base.

5. Place the pumpkin where light can shine through it.

REFLECTIVE HALLOWEEN WAND
(aluminum pie pan, wooden dowel, paper)

1. Punch a hole in the side of an aluminum pie pan. Push a wooden dowel through the hole and to the other side. Glue or tape the dowel in place.

2. Decorate the bottom of the pie pan with paper to create a black cat. Add paper-punch dots around the rim of the pie pan.

NAPKIN HOLDER
(plastic food container, construction paper)

1. Cut a 2-inch section, starting at the top, on each side of a plastic food container, as shown.

2. Use pieces of construction paper to make the outside of the holder look like a pumpkin.

3. Place paper napkins in the cutout section.

LEAF PICTURE
(fallen leaves, construction paper)

1. Select various kinds of leaves, and glue them on a piece of construction paper.

2. Use markers to draw lines around the leaves to create witches, cats, or other Halloween things, and finish the scene.

OWL MOBILE
(lightweight cardboard, brown paper bag, construction paper, yarn, pinecones)

1. Cut an owl head from lightweight cardboard. Cover it with a piece of brown paper bag. Trim around the edges. Add two big round eyes and a triangular beak from construction paper.

2. Punch a hole at the top between the eyes, and add a loop of yarn for a hanger.

3. Glue eyes and a beak on each of four pinecones to make little owls. Glue a piece of yarn to the top of each one.

4. Punch two holes on each side of the big owl's beak. Tie a little owl to each hole.

TRICK-OR-TREAT BAG
(construction paper, large brown paper bag)

1. Glue a half-sheet of construction paper on each wide side of a large brown paper bag, as shown. Let dry.

2. Draw a handle on each piece of paper, across the center of the bag. Cut around the outside and inside of the handles and around the sides of the bag.

3. Use crayons, markers, cut paper, or stickers to decorate the outside of the bag.

TRIANGLES-AND-CIRCLES WITCH
(construction paper, yarn)

1. Cut a triangle from black paper for the witch's body. Cut a circle from light-colored paper for the head.

2. Use a marker to draw a face. Glue on some yarn hair, and glue the head to the body.

3. Cut a smaller black triangle for the hat and glue it on.

4. Cut a big circle from yellow paper for the moon, and glue it in back of the witch.

HOLIDAY PIN
(lightweight cardboard, felt, small bottle tops, safety pin)

1. Cut a shape from lightweight cardboard. Cover it with glue and a piece of felt. Let dry and trim around the edge.

2. Glue small bottle tops on top of the felt. Use felt to decorate the bottle tops as holiday characters.

3. Glue or tape a safety pin to the back.

Paper-Bag Masks

These masks are simple to make using large paper bags. Put your imagination to work, and create something funny or scary, or a favorite animal.

CHICK
(large paper bag, construction paper)

1. Measure about 6 inches from the opening of a large paper bag, and cut around the entire bag. Set aside the cut section.

2. Put the bag on your head. Using a crayon, have a friend carefully mark where the eyeholes should be on the outside of the bag. Remove the bag.

3. Cut out and glue facial features on the chick, but make large eyes. Cut out holes for the eyes. Add curled strips of paper to the top of the chick head.

PUPPY DOG
(large paper bag, construction paper, yarn)

1. Cut off 6 inches from the opening of a large paper bag. Glue construction paper to one large side of the bag.

2. From paper, cut out and glue a head, a nose, a mouth, and two eyes. Add yarn whiskers.

3. Put the bag on your head. Have a friend mark with a crayon where the eyeholes should be. Remove the bag and cut out the eyeholes.

CLOWN
(large paper bag, construction paper, heavy paper plate, poster paint, large plastic bottle top, old newspaper)

1. Cut off 6 inches from the opening of a large paper bag. Set aside the cut section.

2. Put the bag on your head. Using a crayon, have a friend carefully mark where the eyeholes should be on the outside of the bag. Remove the bag. Cut and glue pieces of construction paper to make eyebrows, large eyes with glasses, a nose, a mouth, ears, and a beard. Cut out the eyeholes.

3. Glue a large plastic bottle top in the middle of a painted heavy paper plate. Glue on top of the clown's head.

HIPPOPOTAMUS
(large paper bag, construction paper, crayons, markers)

1. Measure down about 6 inches from the opening of a large paper bag, and cut around the entire bag. Set aside the cut section.

2. Using a piece of light-colored construction paper about the same size as one side of the paper bag, draw the opened mouth of a hippopotamus. Color it with crayons and markers.

3. Glue the hippopotamus face to the paper bag. Put the bag on your head. Using a crayon, have a friend carefully mark where the eyeholes should be on the outside of the bag. Remove the bag and cut out the eyeholes.

4. Add cut-paper flowers around the hippopotamus's head. Trim the bag around the bottom of the head and mouth with scissors.

FROG
(large paper bag, construction paper)

1. Measure about 6 inches from the opening of a large paper bag, and cut around the entire bag. Set aside the cut section.

2. Cover one large side of the paper bag with construction paper, gluing it in place.

3. To make the frog and lily pad, draw and cut pieces from construction paper and glue them in place.

4. Put the bag on your head. Using a crayon, have a friend carefully mark where the eyeholes should be on the outside of the bag. Remove the bag and cut out the eyeholes.

GOBLIN
(large paper bag, rubber band, yarn, construction paper)

1. Cut through the center of the bottom of a large paper bag and along the sides, as shown. Open the flaps. Make fringe with scissors by cutting strips to the folds. Secure the bag below the strips with a rubber band and tie on pieces of black yarn.

2. From construction paper, cut and glue facial features and fringe. With the bag on your head, have a friend carefully mark where the eyeholes should be. Remove the bag and cut out the eyeholes.

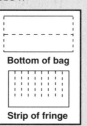

Bottom of bag

Strip of fringe

MATERIAL INDEX

ALUMINUM PIE PAN:
Reflective Halloween Wand....57

BALLOONS:
Cat (Balloon Goblin) 3
Owl (Balloon Goblin)...............3
Papier-Mâché Pumpkin..........21
Pumpkin (Balloon Goblin).......3

BERRY BASKET:
Halloween Berry Basket.........13

BOTTLE TOPS:
Holiday Pin...........................59

BREAD:
Bread-Dough
  Witch Necklace....................11

CARDBOARD:
Ladybug (Special Costume)....33
Owl Mobile 58
Piggy (Hand Mask) 16
Pompon Pumpkin...................26
Three-D Cat...........................41
Tropical Bird (Hand Mask).....16
Witch Pin 52

CARDBOARD BOXES:
Alien (Papier Mâché Mask)...48
Astronaut (Special Costume)..32
Automobile
  (Special Costume) 32
Box Robot (Special Costume)..30
Cereal-Box Clown
  (Special Costume) 30
Christmas Package
  (Special Costume) 34
Elephant (Hand Mask) 17
Ghostly Game 39
Halloween Table Decoration 7
Pumpkin-Seed Box.................55
Sitting Witch 22
Trick-or-Treat Fun Box..........42
Trick-or-Treat Tote 36
Witch (Papier Mâché Mask)...49
Yarn-Covered Witch...............20

**CARDBOARD
CONTAINERS:**
Glittery Bracelets..................25
Halloween Candy Holder........51
Halloween Hang-up 9

Pumpkin Treat Holder...........55

**CARDBOARD
EGG CARTONS:**
Black Cat Mobile....................43
Dancing Goblin......................38
Egg-Carton Pumpkins 14
Egg-Carton Witch 46
Jumping Critter 47

CARDBOARD TUBES:
Cat Napkin Holder..................26
Owl Napkin Holder 42
Pumpkin Napkin Holder 13
Tube Ghost Family 53
Tube Surprise........................54

CELLULOSE SPONGE:
Surprise Jack-o'-Lantern........36

CHALK:
Rub-a-Design..........................19

CHENILLE STICKS:
Ballerina (Special Costume)...31
Fuzzy Spiders 39
Scary Skeleton.......................10

CLOTHES:
Lady and Gentleman
  (Special Costume) 35

CONSTRUCTION PAPER:
Bewitching Eyes.....................29
Black-Cat Stick Puppet 56
Cat Picture 12
Eerie House Card...................42
Funny-Face Pumpkin 40
Ghostly Goggles 22
Halloween Cat........................47
Halloween House 41
Halloween Pop-out Card........27
Halloween Stick Puppet 18
Hanging Bats 28
Haunted-House Card..............8
Leaf Picture 58
Mouse Hat 15
On-Off Pumpkin....................23
Owl Candy Box......................14
Paper Owl..............................25
Pumpkin Bookmark...............47
Pumpkin Card.......................28

Pumpkin Chain 6
Pumpkin Puppet 25
Spooky Picture 19
Triangles-and-Circles Witch...59

CORNCOB:
Corncob Witch 8

CREPE PAPER:
Crepe-Paper Bug....................54

FABRIC:
Fabric Pumpkin Centerpiece..10
Mummy (Special Costume).....30
Scrap-Happy Witch.................12

FELT:
Ghost Pin 7
Witch Finger-Puppet 23

FLOUR:
Bone Necklace 53

FROZEN JUICE LID:
Pumpkin Pin 43

GOURD:
Halloween Gourd 51

ICE-CREAM STICKS:
Wooden-Stick Mummy............39

METAL BANDAGE BOX:
Ghost-in-a-Box 46

MILK CARTONS:
Milk Carton Cat 11
Noisy Goblin 24
Spider and the Web, The 27
Treat Box...............................10

PAPER:
Ghostly Hand Puppet 40
Halloween Banner 36
Spooky Place Card 52

PAPER BAGS:
Bag Owl 13
Boo Treat Bag........................27
Chick (Paper-Bag Mask)........60
Clown (Paper-Bag Mask)........60
Colonial Wig 45

Flashy Jack-o'-Lantern...........44
Frog (Paper-Bag Mask)...........61
Goblin (Paper-Bag Mask) 61
Hippopotamus
    (Paper-Bag Mask) 61
Puppy Dog
    (Paper-Bag Mask) 60
Scarecrow 44
Treat Bags 40
Trick-or-Treat Bag 59
Trick-or-Treat Reflective Bag
   19
Witch Mobile 24

PAPER PLATES:
Bat Hat 9
Bear (Papier-Mâché Mask).....49
Big Eyes 50
Cat (Papier-Mâché Mask).......48
Caterpillar (Hand Mask) 17
Holiday Plate Cover 55
Hooty Owl...............................11
Lion (Special Costume)...........31
Mouse (Papier-Mâché Mask)..49
Panda (Hand Mask)...............17
Paper-Plate Pumpkin 38
Paper-Plate Spider...................7
Party Hat................................50
Pumpkin Decoration 57
Rabbit (Special Costume) 32
Spider Hat 37
Spooky Moon Mobile 6
Sun (Papier-Mâché Mask). 48
Three-Headed Monster
    (Special Costume) 34

PEBBLES:
Pebble Pumpkins 29

PENCILS:
Bat Eraser 44

PLASTIC BOTTLE:
Bottle Witch 15

**PLASTIC
BREAD WRAPPER:**
Ghostly Greetings 45

PLASTIC CONTAINERS:
Glittery Bracelets....................25

Happy Halloween Basket 38
Jack-o'-Lantern Favor 15
Napkin Holder........................58
Pop-out Ghost........................37

PLASTIC-FOAM CUPS:
Goblin Cup.............................37
Goblin Pop-up 9

**PLASTIC-FOAM
EGG CARTON:**
Egg-Carton Bat Branch..........12

PLASTIC-FOAM TRAYS:
Halloween Puzzle....................20
Plastic-Foam Necklace............18

PLASTIC FOOD WRAP:
Spooky See-Through 14

PLASTIC JUGS:
Jingle Ghosts..........................20
Trick-or-Treat Bucket.............22

**PLASTIC
RIBBON HOLDER:**
Spin-a-Web Bracelet 45

POSTER BOARD:
Black-Bean Cat 53
Cat (Hand Mask)....................16
Corny Place Card 21
Five of Hearts
    (Special Costume) 35
Flower (Special Costume).......31
Flying Bat...............................50
Halloween Place Mat 52
Jack-o'-Lantern Spectacles 56
Little Leprechaun
    (Special Costume) 34
Prince (Special Costume)........33
Princess (Special Costume) 33
Scary Black Cat......................21
Spider Card 51
Witch's Hat.............................56

POTATO:
Ghost Stationery 57

PUMPKINS:
Carved Caroline
    (Real Pumpkin Head) 5

Painted Pat
    (Real Pumpkin Head) 4
Sweet Sue
    (Real Pumpkin Head) 4
Topper Dan
    (Real Pumpkin Head) 5
Veggie Vern
    (Real Pumpkin Head) 4
Wendy Witch
    (Real Pumpkin Head) 5

ROCKS:
Rock Crawler..........................23
Rocky Pumpkin 18

SHEET:
Mummy (Special Costume).....30

SOCK:
Cat Hand Puppet 6
Ghost Wind Sock....................26

**SPRING-TYPE
CLOTHESPINS:**
Clothespin Critter 24

STOCKING:
Yarn Hair Wig........................29

TONGUE DEPRESSORS:
Scarecrow Puppet...................54
Tongue Depressor
    Finger Puppets.....................41

TREE BRANCHES:
Goblin Tree............................43
Owl Tree 46

WOODEN DOWEL:
Glittering Wand 28

YARN:
Yarn Jack-o'-Lantern...............8